HOW DOG FOOD SAVED THE EARTH

A tale about everyday, ordinary people

Inspired by a true story

Kory Swanson & Anthony Zolezzi

ASM BOOKS

Kory Swanson & Anthony Zolezzi
How Dog Food Saved the Earth
Copyright © 2005 ASM Books

This is a work of fiction. Any references to historical events, to real people, living or dead, or to real locales are intended only to give the fiction a sense of reality and authenticity. Names, characters, places, and incidents either are the product of the author's imagination or are used fictiously, and their resemblence, if any, to real-life counterparts is entirely coincidental.

For further information contact:

ASM Books
PO Box 3083
La Habra, CA 90631

Printed in Canada

Kory Swanson & Anthony Zolezzi
How Dog Food Saved the Earth

1. Author   2. Title   3. fiction
Library of Congress Control Number: 2005928686
ISBN: 0-9753157-2-2

*To everyday, ordinary people
who work to do the right thing—
may your causes grow and other folks
arrive to lend a helping hand*

Kory would like to thank:

I would not have been able to complete this project without the assistance and encouragement of my wife, Jennifer. Her insightful response and editing made a difficult job much easier. Besides, how often does your wife encourage you to quit your job so you can stay home with the baby and write during naptimes? Thanks Mrs. S!

A great deal of thanks goes out to Mary Jo Swanson for her thoughtful suggestions and careful editing.

To Jeff Todd, Mike Ciecek and Matt Solley, I owe a great deal of thanks also. I'm sure being asked to slog through their buddy's rough manuscript was quite an enticing proposition. I owe you all a lifetime of bike maintenance.

To Anthony, who took a chance asking me to work with him. You'll never know how much this opportunity has meant to me. Thank you.

To all the folks at *Pet Promise*, thank you for being an inspiration.

Anthony would like to thank:

When I look back at all of this, I can't believe how many people, either directly or indirectly, were involved with this project. I think I'd have to write another book just to mention everyone. Thanks to all of you who, in one way or another, contributed to the *Pet Promise* story, and thanks to Kory Swanson for making the story his own and expressing it in a fun and folksy way.

Of course, I couldn't have done any of this without everybody at *Pet Promise* who, behind the scenes, allowed this story to unfold. Special thanks go to Myron Lyskanycz, Dave Carter, Julie Mueller, Curt Gibson, Fred Wynn, Melissa McGinnis, Deb Wurfel, Terry Block, Bill Nicholson, Tom Blair, David Stoup, Larry Yee, and Clark Driftmier.

PART ONE

Prologue

I'd like to tell ya' a little tale. It's a tale I believe is worth tellin'. It's a tale about a handful of everyday, ordinary people, just like you and me, who came together to make the world just a little bit better place to live. These everyday, ordinary people came from far and wide, from different walks of life, not knowin' they had any reason to meet at all. But they did, and that's the story I'm about to tell.

Now, before I go gettin' too far ahead of myself, I'd better introduce ya' to a few of these folks who don't know each other yet. Heck, they don't even know that they're goin' to meet each other, and they sure don't know *why* they're goin' to meet each other. But they will meet 'cause they'll need to, and it won't be 'til then that they'll start to begin to understand it all. And I'm goin' to guess, that it won't be 'til then, or even a little time after that, that you'll start to understand it all too.

Martin

The first everyday, ordinary fella' our story brings us to goes by the name of Martin Trotter. Martin's spent most of his years fumblin' around the food industry. Havin' grown up with a father who caught tuna for a livin' and a grandfather who ran a restaurant, it seemed only fittin' that Martin work with food. Besides, as Martin'll tell ya' if ya' ask, he really likes food.

Now, at age forty-somethin', Martin's logged hundreds, if not thousands, of hours talkin' about food, workin' with food, and helpin' food companies get started. He sure does enjoy all that talkin' and helpin' 'cause he gets a big ol' kick outta' workin' with other people and seein' what kinds of interestin' ideas they come up with when they all put their heads together. Ya' see, our friend Martin here, he's one of those folks who sees the big picture. He ain't real detail oriented, if ya' know what I mean. But, he does seem to understand that everythin' and everyone's connected somehow, which just might be what our li'l ol' story needs from time to time.

When we first meet up with him, however, he's not workin' as a consultant anymore. Ya' see, flyin' from city to city for meetin' after meetin' with company after company'd finally started takin' a toll on Martin and his life outside of work – or shall I say, his lack of it. It'd gotten to the point where he felt all he was doin' was workin'. So, the day his current company called him up, told him he wouldn't have to travel but two times a year, offered a salary and benefits package for a position he felt he'd be able to do in his sleep, and told him he'd work a 9-to-5 week, he jumped at it. He knew he wouldn't be scratchin' his creative itch a whole lot, but he figured he'd live with that as a trade-off, at least for a while. Besides, he'd get to reacquaint himself with his family and maybe actually make it to one of his kid's activities. Shoot, he might even be able to break out that new set of golf clubs his wife bought him two birthdays ago and leave work a little early on Fridays to shoot nine holes. I guess ya' might say our friend, Martin, needed a break. Ya' might also say that our story needs Martin to take a little break, but we'll get to that later. I've got some more introductions to make.

Nick

Our story's second everyday, ordinary fella' goes by the name of Nick Patterson. The mountains in Colorado've been the backdrop to Nick's life, although he's spent more time viewin' them from the eastern Colorado plains than actually roamin' 'em. A stocky, barrel-chested gentleman, Nick can be found most days lookin' out for the welfare of ranchers and farmers. Nick's trademark cowboy hat and boots accompany him wherever he goes and it's well known in the farmin' community that the hat stays on, even for the President.

Nick's spent most of his life followin' a path that he never considered when he was makin' plans to be an adult. Becomin' an agricultural activist just wasn't somethin' he dreamed of doin' as a boy. It definitely wasn't somethin' his folks dreamed of him doin' either, especially since they were the ones footin' the bill for college. They'd hoped for a doctor or a lawyer or even a businessman, but none of those shoes ever seemed to fit Nick. He studied literature, tried his hand at writin' and ended up workin' part-time for a farmers' co-op to pay some bills. It was there that he found somethin' that he really believed in and it was there that he stayed. Besides, he met this cute little farmer's daughter who made it real difficult for him to leave. She was somethin' special and over the next couple of decades would end up bein' one of his biggest supporters, especially when he felt things weren't goin' right. (She's also the only one who knows if Nick ever takes that hat of his off, but there I go again, gettin' sidetracked.)

Nick'd eventually work all over the countryside meetin' farm group after farm group, travelin' to Washington to lobby on behalf of farmers, and even once drivin' his tractor all the way from Colorado to Washington with a bunch of other ticked off farmers who felt the government was doin' 'em more harm than good. Ya' might say Nick held farmers in high esteem. Ya' might say Nick understood farmers. Ya' might also say that he could see the right way to do things and that he didn't much approve of the way farming'd been handled over the years.

Mark

Our story's third everyday, ordinary fella' goes by the name of Mark McClure. From the time he started kindergarten to now, Mark's always been organized. His mama'll tell ya' how he won awards in kindergarten for penmanship. And how he spent hours at recess workin' indoors instead of playin' outside with his friends just so he'd get the letter "G" just right. Or how his bedroom, much to his mama's amazement, was always neat. But we all know how our mamas like to brag…

In college, Mark moved out of his dorm room within the first month and into an efficiency apartment close to campus. He couldn't believe what slobs he was surrounded by. He passed his business courses at the top of his class and was prepared to take his skills into the real world as soon as he could get his hands on his diploma, which, I might add, he earned in three years instead of the typical four. Mark knew there were bigger things out there for him and he had no reason to waste time.

Mark'll enter our story at a time when he's needed, and, it'll just so happen that he'll need our story just as much as it needs him. A successful corporate executive without a job, Mark feels a bit lost, and a bit useless. His wife believes he's havin' a mid-life crisis, although she won't say so. His kids just think he's gettin' old. Job offers've come his way but the hooks've seemed bigger than the bait. Just about nothin' seems to appeal to him right now except for his woodworkin' shop where he hides out and turns rough lumber into beautiful furniture for his friends and family. I guess Mark's just lookin' for somethin' to sink his teeth into. He's looking for somethin' that he can believe in, somethin' that means somethin' more than the bottom line. Mark doesn't know it yet, but he won't have to look much further. In fact, he may not have to look at all. He and his attention to detail're goin' to be needed soon, real soon.

Ben

Our story's fourth everyday, ordinary fella'll be the last one I introduce for quite some time. If I kept introducin' ya' to more folks, ya'd just get confused and I really can't have that now, can I? Benjamin Pollard rounds out our main cast. And, just like Mark, he'll join our story when he's needed. We're goin' to just call him Ben, though. His mama's the only one who ever calls him Benjamin, and that's only when she's angry.

Anyway, what can I say about Ben? Well, Ben happens to be one of those fellas who always seems to be just a bit too uptight. The man just can't seem to relax. He wasn't relaxed the day he entered the world, the day he started school, or the day he enrolled in college. And he sure didn't relax after college. When he took his first entry-level position at one of New York city's premier marketin' firms he moved through the ranks in record time. With Ben on the payroll, the firm was forced to expand. He brought in so many new clients that at one point his boss told him to slow down. The rest of the company couldn't keep up. Ya' see, Ben's a mover and a shaker. He doesn't know how to sit still for very long. When he sees somethin' he wants he goes after it. Early on in his career, he went after money and overall, ya' might say he did rather well for himself. The European sports car, the expensive suits, the designer shoes, and the Rolex have no problem lettin' ya' know that Ben's financial situation isn't one the rest of us'd probably turn our backs on.

But now, as Ben reaches his late 40's, his hair thins out a bit, and his kids get closer to college, he feels like he needs to be doin' somethin' other than chasin' greenbacks. Of course, like the rest of our cast, he has no idea that he's a part of this story or that he'll even get mixed up with the likes of Martin, Nick, and Mark. But he does know he needs a change and the experience and knowledge that he'll bring to the group'll sure be helpful when he finally arrives. The guys just might need someone to give 'em a little extra push, or tow 'em along behind him, if that's what it takes.

ᘔ ⑥ ᘔ

So ya've met Martin, our idea man. Ya've met Nick, our farm activist. Ya've met Mark, our keep it neat and orderly organizer, and last, but certainly not least, ya've met Ben, our mover and shaker. Ya'd be right to assume that you'll be meetin' each one of these fellas in the order they're introduced. That's just how the story goes. Anyway, we'll meet a few more folks later but I'd better stop right here with the introductions for now. I sure don't want to overwhelm ya'. There's time for that later. Besides, I don't want ya' to feel like ya've just been at some big party where ya've shook a hundred hands and ya' can't remember any of the folks who're attached to those hands.

So for now, I'd better just get on with the story. I sure do hope ya' like it.

Chapter 1

A few years back, on a hot summer day in Southern California, Martin Trotter found his six-foot-three frame casting a long shadow in a berry patch. No ordinary berry patch, mind you, but a large berry patch. The largest patch of strawberries that Martin had ever set eyes on, let alone set foot in. Row after row of perfectly planted strawberries stretched from one end of the horizon to the other. And berry after juicy berry begged to be picked from these luscious green plants and plopped into his mouth. Memories of boyhood crept back into Martin's thoughts: sitting at his mother's kitchen table, dipping a finger into the whipped cream his mother had lavished on top of his strawberry shortcake, sneaking into his grandparents' garden and sneaking off with a handful of his grandpa's coveted strawberries, even agreeing to wash all the windows on the outside of the house in the middle of a hot summer day just so he could get his strawberry sundae before his brothers and sister. Martin sure liked strawberries. And now, here he stood in the middle of the largest strawberry patch he'd ever imagined, both puzzled and in awe at the same time.

Liking strawberries, however, was about the only thing Martin knew about them which is why he was puzzled when the company sent him out on this assignment. He knew that a strawberry pastry puff sat on a shelf back at the home office waiting to hit the market just as soon as the company could line up a strawberry supplier, but he didn't know why they'd sent him. So far, every strawberry supplier had wanted too much money and Martin's company just wasn't going to be able to make the kind of profit on each bar that they needed to. In fact, they were about to shelve the whole project. As a last resort, the company decided to send Martin to meet with a new strawberry producer to try and negotiate a deal. The company wanted to cut out the middle man and felt it would be in their best interest to send someone other than their normal buyer, someone who held a little clout in the company, to go and make the first impression and possibly work out a deal. As the company's Director of Western States, the privilege fell to Martin. He guessed they thought he knew something about strawberries, so rather than contradict them, he had decided he'd go out and do his best. He had faked his way through many meetings over the years. How difficult could it be to go and look at a bunch of strawberries? He would make the best of it and enjoy his day out of the office. A day driving through the countryside away from the riff-raff of traffic and the white noise of the office sounded pleasant. So now, at 8:30 a.m., here he stood, knee deep in strawberry plants prepared and yet unprepared to check out this strawberry producer's operation. Little did Martin know that this short visit to the strawberry patch, this insignificant day trip out to the farmlands, would send his life and his career down an entirely new path. A new path that Martin never envisioned for himself. A new path that had never been part of his life plan. A new path that would ultimately lead him towards something good, something really good.

After a half-hour meeting walking the rows of strawberries with the field manager, Martin understood more about strawberry preparation, growth, and production than he cared to ever know. He was relieved. He never had to act like he knew anything about strawberries. The field manager went right ahead and filled him in on everything, except for one thing. The only thing that he hadn't done yet was offer Martin some strawberries to taste. And after walking around in the hot sun for thirty minutes, and only having had a cup of coffee for breakfast, Martin wanted to know just how good these strawberries tasted. Would the field manager let him take some home for dessert tonight? He hadn't had good strawberry shortcake in a long time. Besides, he could skip the whip cream, he told himself. Keeping fit was a bit more difficult these days. Somewhere along the way he had traded in his tall, lean, I-can-eat-anything body for one that was a bit more soft around the edges. The previous month, he'd made it a goal of his to watch his food intake. But, as he stood and looked out over those strawberries, his meeting with the field manager coming to an end, the thought of strawberry shortcake wouldn't go away.

"Would you mind, terribly, if I helped myself to a couple of strawberries?" Martin asked the field manager as he bent down and plucked a couple off of the nearest bush.

"No, I don't mind, take as many as you want. But I wouldn't eat any of 'em if I were you."

"But these strawberries are beautiful. They're perfect," Martin replied.

"They might look pretty and they may seem perfect, but they're sprayed with chemical pesticides and herbicides."

"But I love strawberries. I've eaten them my whole life and these might just be the best looking strawberries I've ever seen."

"Looks can be mighty deceiving. It's what you don't see that's the problem. It's the stuff we spray on 'em."

"Why? What kind of stuff do you spray?"

"We spray pesticides. We spray herbicides. We spray for anything that might hinder the growth of the strawberry plants. You know, weeds and beetles and caterpillars. We pretty much kill anything that isn't a strawberry plant. And since we kill off everything in the ground, even the good stuff, we have to also spray chemical fertilizers so that the strawberries grow big and are more profitable for the company."

"So these strawberries are covered in chemicals?"

"Yep. We just sprayed yesterday."

"But I don't see anything."

"It dries clear."

"I suppose all this chemical spray isn't meant to be ingested by humans either."

"That's for sure. I get to take all the free strawberries home with me that I want, but I don't take any. I don't want to give my family and friends this stuff. Heck, the company makes us wear protective clothing when we spray. They don't want us coming back and suing them in 10 years for some strange disease we contracted from breathing this stuff. That's why I don't want my kids eating these strawberries. Heck, I don't even really want them eating any strawberries from anywhere. I haven't eaten a strawberry in several years."

"Then why do you use all this stuff?"

"It increases the strawberry yield and it makes the strawberries look wonderful. The company can then sell more at a greater price."

"But it doesn't seem right."

"No, I guess it doesn't seem right."

"Besides, I'm sure your company doesn't make sure all of those chemicals don't get washed away after a rain. How many people and animals do they end up hurting?"

Martin dropped the strawberry on the ground and wiped his hand on his khakis. He had to remember to wash his hands as soon as he could. He had thought he'd seen everything he needed to see and been prepared to leave, but now he wanted to see more. He wanted to get a real close look at what was going on here at the strawberry patch. As he continued walking through the strawberry plants he was careful not to touch anything. He did, however, make mental notes of everything and he sure didn't like what he saw.

Now Martin was no botanist, but he could tell things weren't right. As a boy, he'd spent enough time playing around his grandparents' garden to know what looked right and what didn't. And one thing he knew for sure, there were supposed to be bugs. There were always supposed to be plenty of bugs, but in this strawberry field, Martin hadn't set his eyes on one. The summer sun beat down on the field but no bees, no butterflies, not even a fly darted about in the air. Not one single, solitary ant crawled on the ground. Strange. The soil looked funny too, almost oily. It looked as if someone had dumped cans of motor oil everywhere. It sure didn't look like his grandpa's garden. This soil looked dead. When Martin dug into the ground with the heel of his shoe to take a closer look he found nothing. No worms, no beetles, no signs of life. Things sure didn't seem right and Martin had seen enough. He needed to get away from these strawberries, and he wasn't sure he'd ever eat another one for the rest of his life.

Martin thanked the berry patch supervisor for his time and headed to his car. He had a new dilemma on his hands now. *What am I going to tell my company?* Martin wondered. He knew that his conscience wasn't going to allow him to tell the company it was okay to use these strawberries. *I can't put chemically-treated strawberries into pastry puffs. I just can't do it. But what do I tell the company? The pastry puffs are ready for production. What are they going to say? If they say they still want to get strawberries from this producer can I keep working for them?* Martin's thoughts raced. He sure didn't know what he was going to do.

やや ⑥ やや

Ya' know, I find this part of our story to be a bit funny. Not funny in the laughin' sense, just funny in the strange sense. Ya' see, Martin, who's spent his entire life around food, has just realized he knows very little about modern day farm production. Sure, he'd sold food products, started up restaurant chains, and consulted with folks far and wide, but farmin' wasn't an area he ever really paid much attention to. He'd never had any cause to worry about the farms because the food that he sold'd already gone through one form of processin' or another and was far removed from the farm by the time he came across it.

Ya' see, like most of us, Martin's been sleepin' through his meals and his wife's meals and his kids' meals. He assumed, I guess like most of us do, that the powers that be were lookin' out for Mr. and Mrs. Everybody and their families. Isn't that what they get paid to do? Aren't there people in high places who have a responsibility to protect the public? Maybe that's just a little too logical for some folks to understand, especially now that we've all visited the strawberry patch with Martin.

Well now, there sure seems to be a problem at hand, don't ya' agree? Shoot, if Martin didn't know any of this – and remember, Martin'd worked in the food industry for over 20 years – who did?

Chapter 2

As Martin drove his car out of the dusty parking lot at the strawberry field, he decided he would head back towards a town he'd driven through earlier that day. He'd seen a couple of little diners and decided to stop at one of them and eat a quiet lunch. Lunch, however, would turn out to be anything but quiet. As he ate, his thoughts filled with visions of overgrown, chemically treated strawberries being nurtured by men in chemical suits marching up and down row after row of strawberry plants. He still couldn't believe someone would sell chemically treated fruit to people. He thought about all the strawberries his two children had eaten in their short lives and hoped he hadn't done anything to harm them in the long run. He knew they wouldn't be eating strawberries any time soon.

As his lunch wound down and he got ready to go, the waitress came over to give him his check.

"Is everythin' alright, honey? You havin' a bad day? You look like you could use some of our homemade strawberry shortcake. It's the best shortcake around."

"No, thanks. I don't think I can stand the sight of even a single strawberry right now." Martin replied.

"You don't like strawberries? Who in their right mind doesn't like strawberries? Oh, you've just got to try our strawberry shortcake. It'll change your mind for good. You'll bring the whole family back. Let me go and get you one. It'll be on the house."

"No thanks, really. I used to love strawberries, but after my visit to the strawberry fields this morning, I don't think I'll ever eat them again."

"What happened at the strawberry field this morning?" the waitress asked.

"Do you have any idea what kind of stuff those people spray on their strawberries?"

"You bet I do. And now, I see the problem. You just didn't go to the right strawberry field."

"What do you mean?" Martin asked.

"Well, you see, around here there are two types of strawberry fields – those that spray and those that don't. Unfortunately, most of the strawberry fields around here spray, but a few don't. We locals only go to the strawberry fields that don't. I can give you directions to the best one around if you'd like."

Martin's spirits perked up a bit, "Directions would be great. It would be nice to see some strawberry plants that won't frighten me."

"Oh, you'll like it out there. And the strawberries are delightful. Now are you sure I can't get you some of our famous strawberry shortcake?"

Well, that depends. Are the strawberries on your strawberry shortcake from a place that doesn't spray?"

"Well of course, honey. They come from the same field I'll be sendin' you to after lunch. And I think that sounds like a, "Yes, ma'am, I'd love some of your strawberry shortcake." Let me go and get you some right away." With that, the waitress turned and headed into the kitchen before Martin could respond. In no time she returned and placed fresh strawberry shortcake mounded with whip cream on his table along with directions to the strawberry farm. "We make the shortcake and the whipped cream here from scratch, also. Enjoy. And thanks for stoppin' in. Hope to see you back here some time soon."

Martin thanked the woman, ate his delicious strawberry shortcake, paid his check, and headed to his car, directions to the strawberry farm tucked inside his shirt pocket.

ॐ ⑥ ॐ

Who'd've ever thought that Martin's short little trip to a small town diner would turn into a learnin' session? And who'd've ever thought that the waitress, who'd probably been walkin' those floors for years, would end up bein' the teacher? Ya' see, we never really know when we're goin' to learn somethin' or who we're goin' to learn it from. Maybe we shouldn't turn a blind eye or a deaf ear to those we think have nothin' to offer. After all, Martin walked out of the place with a whole new attitude. In the half hour or so that he sat in that vinyl red booth, he went from a disgruntled, hater of strawberries to someone who found some hope, to someone who found out that there just might be a different way to grow strawberries. Wouldn't it be nice if he were able to work a contract for his company with the farm he was headin' to. He'd just have to wait and see.

Chapter 3

Martin drove back through the countryside. As he drove, his disgust changed into excitement. "There's a better way." Martin said aloud. There definitely was a better way. At least that's what the waitress said. Martin didn't know much about farming but what he did know, was that farming had been around since the beginning of time – way before chemical fertilizers and herbicides and pesticides. When he was a kid his grandparents' had a huge garden and their plants had grown without chemicals. His grandpa used to drag him out to the garden to pull weeds and keep the garden healthy. The only thing he ever saw his grandpa spray on the garden was water. If plants could grow on a small scale like his grandparents garden, then surely things could grow on a greater scale without all the pesticides and herbicides.

Having worked in the food industry since he left college, Martin was a bit surprised that he had more to learn. In fact, he had a lot to learn. He knew next to nothing about the cultivation of fruits and vegetables. He had never needed to. Now, it turned his stomach to think that he probably sold food grown with pesticides and herbicides through his business transactions over the years. Initially, he began selling food because he liked it. He also liked it because he felt like he had a hand in feeding folks, which to him seemed a bit more important than selling cars or appliances. Now, as he cruised along the backroads he wasn't so sure he could continue down the same path. In fact, Martin decided from that moment on that he was going to do something different. He didn't care what he had to do, but he refused to sell any more food that came from producers who used chemicals. People deserved healthy food and he was going to deliver it to them.

Rounding a bend, Martin saw the sign for the strawberry patch – "Little Valley Organic Strawberries – 3 miles ahead." *Organic strawberries? Uh, oh. Some weirdo, peace lovin' throwback from the 60's must be running this place,* Martin thought. The organics movement was largely considered the red-headed stepchild of the food industry. Mainstream industry people often joked about the organics movement. They were a tiny, little blip on the national food industry's radar and the folks involved were often seen as fanatics. Besides, only hippies and vegetarians bought organic food. As he pulled into the long dusty driveway, Martin wondered how this strawberry farm did things differently. He also wondered what kind of character ran the place. Would he be wasting his time if he stopped in? Looking at his watch, he saw that the day was getting on. The fact that this was an 'organic' farm almost made him turn around and head home but something in the back of his head made him steer his car up the driveway and check things out.

As he put the car in park and opened his door, he decided to head for the shed with the "Office" sign above the door. *No peace signs yet,* he thought to himself, *Just a friendly looking younger guy in a plaid shirt and khakis stepping outside to greet me. He's not who I was expecting.*

"Good afternoon. Can I help you with anything today?"

"I hope so. I'm interested in your strawberries and how they're grown. Do you think you can help me?

"I've been growing strawberries since I was old enough to carry a bucket. My father grew them on this farm, but he just retired. I took over the operation when he left, but he still checks in on me just about every day. What would you like to know?"

"Would you mind showing me around?"

"I'd be more than happy to show you around. You looking for anything in particular?"

"I'm not sure. I think so."

"Well c'mon then. I'll help you look for what you don't know you're looking for," the young farmer said with a smile.

No patchouli oil, no love beads, no tie-dye, no folk songs. This guy looks like a regular farmer, Martin thought to himself.

As he followed the farmer out to the rows and rows of strawberries, it didn't take long to see that this field was quite different than the lifeless, oily, chemically altered strawberry field he had visited earlier. He was delighted to see bugs flitting about. He couldn't remember the last time he was actually happy to see a fly, but oddly enough, it seemed to put him at ease. As the young farmer bent down and picked a few strawberries, Martin shuddered. Visions of men in chemical suits holding perfect strawberries in their rubber-gloved hands flashed through his mind again. When the farmer popped one in his mouth and handed a couple towards Martin, he hesitated.

"What's the matter? You don't like strawberries?"

"No. I love strawberries, but the farm I visited this morning sprayed their plants and their soil with chemicals. I've kind of lost my appetite for strawberries. Even the guy that showed me around that farm told me not to eat the strawberries. I guess that's why I'm here. The waitress at the diner sent me. She said you don't spray your strawberries, and she gave me some of her short-cake with strawberries from your farm and well… "

"So, that's why you are interested in my farm? You had to love Linda's strawberry shortcake. In fact, I'm heading into town later today. I might just have to stop in and have some of her short-cake, especially since she's puttin' in a good word about me. I'm glad she sent you here. I'm always looking for a reason to talk about my strawberries."

Martin popped a strawberry in his mouth. It was delicious. "Do you mind if I have another?"

The young farmer chuckled, "You go right ahead. I don't think I'm going to run out any time soon. And now that I've got you tasting them, why don't I tell you a little bit about them. As far as I know, and as far back as my dad can remember, the only thing that's ever been put on this soil has been natural. We've never used chemicals on our plants or anything artificial for that matter. And, we never will as long as I run this farm. Besides, we really can't because we're an organic farm. A special sticker from the U.S. Department of Agriculture goes on all of our berries and each season we get inspected to prove that we don't use chemicals. I'd be out of business if I started using all of that stuff. I get a good price for my strawberries being organic. I can't sell my strawberries as organic if I use chemicals, and if I did, I'd have to compete with the big factory farms who spray. All those chemicals allow them to grow their berries more efficiently which lets them set their prices low. As it is, I can only stay in business because my strawberries fetch a higher price because they aren't chemically treated. Organic fruits and vegetables only account for a small slice of the market, but any food that states that it is organic has to be grown without chemicals. Fortunately, there are enough folks who are willing to pay a bit extra because they like to know that their food is fresh and clean.

"I have a lot to learn," Martin sighed. "You know, I've been in the food business for most of my life. How come I don't know any of this"

"Unfortunately, most people don't. Most consumers don't take much time to educate themselves. If it's on the shelves at the store, they buy it."

"I guess you're probably right. It's a little scary though."

"That's one of the reasons I'm always willing to talk about my strawberries. Hopefully I can help people like you understand some things."

"I'd sure like to understand more. Would you mind if I dig into your ground a little bit?"

"Sure," the young farmer replied. "What are you looking for?"

"Worms. Bugs. Anything living."

"You'll find plenty of those. This soil is rich and the bugs and worms help keep it that way. Here, take a look." The farmer dug into the soil with his hands and pulled up a good clump of soil. It was the type of soil that reminded Martin of his grandparent's garden. It looked fresh and alive. A worm wiggled in the farmer's hand.

"Are you going fishing any time soon? These chubby little worms make the bass go crazy," the farmer said with a twinkle in his eyes.

"No thanks. I haven't been fishing in years. Although, that's a pretty healthy looking worm, maybe I'll eat him." The farmer and

Martin both laughed. It was the first time since the morning that Martin had actually chuckled about something. "Do you suppose you can explain more about what you mean when you talk about 'organic' farming? How does it differ from other farming?"

"Well, it's essentially responsible farming. Organic farming makes sure that the land remains sustainable year after year. It treats each one of the necessary components – the soil, the water, the air and the plants – with equal importance. Most bigger, corporate farms treat the product – the fruit or the vegetable or the meat – as the most important part. On an organic farm we know that we can't separate everything out that neatly. Take my farm for instance, strawberry plants need healthy, fertile soil. If I neglect the soil by spraying a bunch of pesticides my strawberry plants will weaken. The worms and other insects that help keep the soil aerated and fertile will die and the soil will lose all of its nutrients. Once that happens, I'd have to use chemical fertilizers to make the soil usable again. Pretty soon, with fertilizers offsetting the pesticides and vice versa, the plants become addicted to the sprays. The more a farmer sprays, the more he has to spray because along with killing the pests, he kills all the healthy things too. Essentially, the soil sort of dies. It is tempting to spray, though. Chemical pesticides and herbicides seem like a blessing at first. You get good crops, the bugs don't eat your fruit, and you don't have to worry about weeds choking off your plants. But when it comes down to it, they really create a vicious cycle of dependency which in the long run may destroy the soil and the nearby water sources. You need soil that is diverse and full of life to grow good healthy crops. Farmers have depended on the natural cycles of things for ages and that's, I guess, what we're still trying to do. Besides, I want to know that the food I produce is good for people. I just wouldn't feel right if I sold chemically sprayed food to folks."

"But doesn't farming this way make you less competitive in the marketplace?"

"Unfortunately, yes. I have to work harder to make a profit. There is, however, a growing market for organic foods. The growth is slow, consumers need to be educated, and most large grocery stores don't want to do business with a small farm like me, but we're gaining ground. In fact, one of the ways is through farmer's markets. I bet there's one in your area each week. You should go and check it out."

"So why do you do it? Why do you go the extra mile and make less money in the end?"

"It's the right thing to do. The way I see it, farmers, are the caretakers of the earth. Everything I do on the farm has a consequence. Maybe not for me in the immediate future, but maybe for my children or the children down the road. I don't want to contaminate my soil, or my groundwater, or the nearby streams. I want my community livable for years to come. I'd love to pass this land on just as my dad did to me."

"Do other farms, not just strawberry farms, use chemicals also?"

"They sure do. There are a number of us who farm organically. We all believe in what we do and we try to work together to help each other out. Our numbers are slowly growing."

"I can't believe that the government allows farms to spray so many different chemicals on food and sell it. It just doesn't seem right."

"We can't seem to get the lawmakers to see it that way, but we keep trying. Corporate lobbyists have a lot of money to help push policies through in Washington."

Martin had seen all that he needed to see. He thanked the young farmer for his tour, purchased a flat of fresh strawberries and headed to the car. As he drove away, he felt relieved. There was another way to grow strawberries, a better way. In fact, there was a better way to grow all sorts of fruits and vegetables. He was relieved to know that there were people out there who cared about the food they put on other people's tables.

จ๋ ⑥ จ๋

What'd begun as a quiet drive into the country and a day out of the office'd turned into somethin' Martin could'nt've predicted. Like most of us, Martin was brought up bein' taught to do what was right, and other than a few foolish mistakes here and there, the kind we all make from time to time, Martin'd spent most of his life doin' the right thing. So, now that he'd been exposed to farmin' in the chemical sense and farmin' in the organic sense, he knew he had to make some changes. He wasn't sure just what those changes were goin' to look like, but he knew somethin' had to be done. He knew the first place he could try to make changes would be in his company. He knew, however, that bringin' up organic foods would most likely cause some tension at the office.

Sometimes though, when a person's driven by a force bigger than themselves, it just doesn't matter if it leads to some tension and disagreements. Often times, we just have to experience a bit of discomfort for somethin' good to happen. And sometimes that little bit of discomfort just doesn't matter, especially when you believe ya're doin' the right thing. In this case, Martin knew that he had to do the right thing, even if it would make some waves.

Chapter 4

Martin was a little wound up the moment he arrived home. His wife had no idea where this man, ranting and raving about pesticides and herbicides and organic food, had come from. Wasn't he supposed to be taking a nice quiet drive through the countryside today? Shouldn't he be calm and relaxed? It took a little while to get him settled down enough to actually start from the beginning, but when he finally came up for air, she knew things were going to change. She'd seen that look in his eye before. It was a look that told her he'd found something to sink his teeth into, a determined look. This time, though, he sounded more determined than he had in a long time. Martin also informed her that she could only purchase organic foods from now on. The extra cost wouldn't matter in the long run if it kept the family healthy. Besides, every organic product they purchased would help out a farmer who was working to do the right thing.

Martin's wheels spun. As soon as he could get himself into his office and onto his computer, the research began. The consultant inside him awoke from its hibernation. He wanted to call the vice president and tell him all that he had found. He wanted to tell him that the company could only use organic strawberries in their new pastry puff. He wanted to tell him that they could only use organic foods in all of their products, that they had an obligation as a company to do the right thing and to sell healthy food. *Hold on a second Martin,* he thought to himself as he sat at his computer. *Slow down. Take a deep breath and take a step back. What do you really want out of all of this?*

Martin had asked himself a good question. Ultimately, he'd love to see his company change all of their food production over to organics. In fact, he'd love to see every food company change over to organics. *Imagine the ripple effect organics would have throughout the farming community!* Martin thought. *Imagine the positive effect organics would have on the environment! Imagine the positive effects they would have at dinner tables across the land!*

Of course, all of these things sounded wonderful, but Martin had worked in corporate America long enough to know that it would be hard to sell any of this to his company.

I know I'm getting carried away, but I've got to think big. Martin took a deep breath. *Okay, what can I do right now?* he asked himself.

Early the next morning, Martin emerged from his office tired but energized. He had stayed up all night drafting a proposal to his company. The company would start a new division, an organic food division devoted strictly to the production of healthy, organic alternatives for everyday people. They would allow him to run it, hire his own people, and try to make it successful. If the division didn't achieve success a year from now, he'd resign and the company could dissolve the division. If the division, however, became a success, the company would have a foothold in an entirely new market. Martin believed the company had nothing to lose.

Over breakfast, Martin looked back at the past 24 hours. *It sure is amazing how quickly some things can change the way you think and feel,* he thought. He had learned a lot and was bound and determined to start making changes as soon as possible even though he knew he had a lot more to learn. He had barely scratched the surface but the little voice inside him, the one that had first spoken to him yesterday afternoon, kept telling him that he had to follow this new path. He had to spread the word about organic foods even though he knew it wouldn't be easy. As he headed out to his car, all he could hope was that his company would see things his way.

Unfortunately, it didn't. By 10 a.m. on the Monday of the following week, Martin turned in his resignation. He had spoken at length with the vice president, who, even after Martin shared him his plan, thought Martin couldn't be serious. He wouldn't even consider his proposal. When Martin went over his head and made an appointment with the company president, he got a call back the following day stating that the president wouldn't be available to speak with him after all. The vice president had obviously sent word and blocked any chance that Martin would have to pitch his idea. Martin had run into the brick wall of corporate America, one that wanted only to make a quick profit and answer positively to its shareholders each quarter. One that he knew would never listen to him or want to work with him. Martin remembered why he had been a consultant for so long. He had avoided this type of treatment for years because whenever something went sour he had always been able to walk away. There had always been a new project waiting in the wings.

꒐ ⑥ ꒐

So yes, Martin read the writin' on the wall. He knew he had to go find other folks who'd be more willin' to work with him. It might take years for his company to pursue organics. Shoot, it might be never. And, even with the uncertainty of havin' no job lined up, Martin knew he had to go find other folks who could help him with his new cause.

Of course, leavin' a stable job with great benefits and a great schedule's never an easy thing to do, especially when the future is cloudy. But, none of that mattered to Martin. He knew that there'd always be a way for him to make a livin'. He knew it wouldn't take him long to find somethin' to do that would allow him to pursue his new found cause and to earn a livin'. He knew there were like-minded folks out there workin' with organic food who'd welcome someone with his knowledge and experience in the food industry. Ya' see, even though Martin was a bit uneasy about all of this, he still felt at peace. He felt at peace 'cause he knew there'd be a place for him. And that place'd allow him to work to make the earth a better place to live.

Chapter 5

Jobless and entering new territory, Martin felt a bit uneasy. His uneasiness, however, was offset by his desire to make an impact, and he channeled the added stress and discomfort into his work. Ramping up his research into organic and sustainable farming, Martin spent hours contacting people. Even after 20 some years in the food industry, he didn't really know many people who worked with organic food. If he was going to make any progress, he needed to build a solid network of people who could help. If he was going to find success he had to be able to get his consultant name out into the field. Any phone call or email that he sent might lead to something positive. The research he completed was exhaustive and he made it clear to whomever he spoke that he would consult primarily with companies who were using organic food sources or making a strong attempt to move in that direction. He learned as much as he could about pesticides, herbicides, and chemical fertilizers and found studies about the residual effects of foreign substances in foods. He looked at food preservatives, food additives, sugar substitutes, and dyes. The more he discovered, the more concerned he became. Much of the food that the general public purchased was grown using synthetic, unnatural ingredients.

In terms of farming, Martin began to see a pattern with the organic approach. Most of the farms involved in sustainable, organic farming were small operations, owned and operated by families. Often times these small farms banded together and formed alliances, co-ops, in order to share resources and grab a larger market share. But, even the most successful co-ops still had a difficult time competing with the endless financial resources of the factory farms. In fact, looking at it from a business standpoint, Martin wondered why the organic farmers and producers did it. *Why bother farming at all? It's hard work. It's hard to make a living. And, it's hard to raise a family. Besides, how do they ever make any sort of profit when the market is so small?*

In the weeks and months to come, Martin learned more and more as he networked with others involved in the organic food industry. He also began speaking with the owners of small family farms. He never realized how proud most farmers were. It was a pride that came from a deep, long-lasting history as part of the national landscape. Farmers with ties to countries all over the world had settled the wild American countryside and made it flourish. They had paved the way for the future of all Americans and the family farmers who Martin spoke with had a lot of pride in that history. Essentially, they had fed a country and it grew strong.

Even still, with all the farming history behind them, Martin couldn't figure out why anyone would want to farm. The day-to-day grind of being a farmer was hard work – livestock got sick, market prices fluctuated, the weather didn't like to cooperate. So why did they do it? And why had these farmers embraced sustainable, organic farming methods when modern technology would make things easier on them?

As it turns out, many of the farmers that Martin contacted viewed themselves as caretakers of the earth. Martin remembered back to the day in the organic strawberry field when the young farmer had told him pretty much the same thing. Farmers understand that future generations will need healthy land. Sustainable farming encourages diverse farming practices that allow the soil to be viable year after year. It also keeps the nearby streams, rivers, and groundwater clean. Sustainable farms remain healthy, livable places where children can grow into healthy responsible citizens. The farmers who farm them understand that they are a part of a community and that the overall health of the community depends on them doing the right thing. The food they produce must be healthy. They can't imagine selling chemically treated food. They value their own families and community too much. As the young strawberry farmer, early on, had relayed to him, Martin learned that the small family farmer takes great care to farm responsibly because it is the right thing to do.

⌇ ⑥ ⌇

Sometimes, people ya' think ya' know, just don't turn out to be who ya' think they are. Martin grew up in the city and suburbs. He didn't know much about country life and he didn't know much about farmers. He considered them to be simple, close-minded, uneducated, country folk who didn't know much about anythin'. Boy, he'd learned he was wrong. The stereotypes he'd latched onto sure missed the target. Instead of a bunch of Willie-Nelson-lis-tenin', buck-toothed, overall-clad, shotgun totin' neanderthals, Martin found warmth. He found a group of everyday, ordinary people whose goals in life were similar to his own. They wanted to raise their families well, see their children grow into successful adults, and make sure their time on this planet'd be remembered positively. They're hardworkin', give-ya'-the-shirt-off-their-backs folks, the kind who'd leave the warmth of their homes in the mid-dle of an icy snowstorm to help a stranded motorist on the inter-state in the middle of who-knows-where Iowa or Nebraska.

So ya' see, Martin finally learned somethin' that'd stick with him the rest of his life. He learned somethin' we've all got to learn. And, yes, I know it might sound a bit cliché, and ya' may've heard it a few times before, but I don't think we've all taken it to heart yet. Ya' see, there're a lot of good people out there, and they may look or act a bit differently, but, ya' might never get to understand 'em if ya' never take the time to really learn about 'em. After all, most of us're good people, whether we come from the biggest city or the smallest town. And, believe it or not, most of us want to do what's right, just like our good friend, Martin.

Chapter 6

One sunny afternoon, a few months into his research, Martin drove to an appointment with a rancher who raised cattle using natural feed. He had discovered that sustainable farming wasn't only limited to fruits and vegetables. The comparisons between factory farm beef production and natural beef production were startling, especially when it came to protein supplements, antibiotic treatments, and bovine growth hormone usage. Martin wanted to know from a rancher in the industry, what the big deal was in terms of antibiotics and hormones. Besides, a trip to a natural beef ranch would add to his ever-growing network of sustainable farmers and organic industry contacts.

Martin never knew what to expect on visits like these, but he'd learned not to jump to any conclusions before he had a chance to get to know someone. As he drove up the long, dusty driveway, a round-faced, white-haired gentleman dressed in tan work clothes waved for him to stop. As the older man ambled up to the car, Martin could barely make out the patch on the farmer's well-worn, green and white mesh hat but it looked to be the logo of a prominent national natural feed distributor. Martin turned off the car and reached over to grab his notebook and pen. As he turned back towards the drivers' side door, it opened and Martin found himself looking up at a rather rotund belly hidden behind a tan workshirt, a large hand extended in his direction.

"Ya' must be Martin Trotter," the workshirt and hand seemed to say. "Been expectin' ya'. Glad to know ya'. I'm William Newhouse. Most people just call me Bill."

Climbing out of his car, Martin shook hands, "Nice to meet you, Mr. Newhouse. I have a meeting with a Thomas Newhouse. Are you his father?"

"Certainly am. Tommy's my boy. He took over for me a few years ago when my back started actin' up. After that, the rest of my body started followin' suit. I just can't work like I used to so Tommy, he handles most of the farm operations 'round here these days. Earlier this mornin' he got called into town for a bit so he asked me to show ya' 'round and answer any questions ya' might have. I sure do hope that's gonna be okay."

"Of course, of course. Thank you, Mr. Newhouse."

"Now that's the second time you've done that. Won't ya' please just call me Bill?" he said with a twinkle in his eye.

"Alright Bill," Martin smiled, "What can you tell me about the operation here?"

"Well, I can tell ya' quite a bit. Where do ya' want me to start?

"Well, I guess I'm looking for as much information as I can get about natural beef production and family ranch life. I'd also like to know what your take is on the use of antibiotics and growth hormones in cattle production. I've spent a lot of time the past few months learning about organic food production and sustainable farming, but most of what I've learned has been about fruits and vegetables. It's time I learned about meat and dairy and that's what brought me to you."

"Ye'r sure tearin' off a huge chunk of information. I can help ya' with the beef questions and general farmin' questions, but I won't be much good with the dairy stuff. Never did like milkin' cows much. Ye'r better off goin' and visitin' a dairy farm. I can give ya' a few names of places when ya' leave if ya'd like."

"I'd like that very much. Thank you. Would you like to sit down before we get started?"

"That sounds like a pretty good idea. It sure is a beauty of a day, why don't we sit right over there on that bench under that old oak tree and I'll do the talkin' until Tommy gets back. He can show ya' 'round. I'm not much good at gettin' 'round the barns and the gates and the fences these days.

Bill led Martin over to the bench which had been placed to give off a view of the rolling green countryside. Martin was glad to be sitting in the shade. It was a beautiful day, but the sun was getting pretty hot.

"Now, let's see. Let's see...where should I start? I guess I might as well just dive in and if ya' think of anythin' specific, just ask. I'll start with a little farm history 'cuz most folks don't know much about farmers. After that, we'll talk about cattle."

"That's fine with me. I'll stop you if I need to. The more information I can get the more it will help me understand.

"Ya' certainly are easy to get along with, aren't ya'?" Bill joked. "Did ya' know there's been farms just about as long as there's been people? Well, it's true. Folks've been farmin' for hundreds of years..."

As the old rancher began, Martin felt like he had struck gold. He was out there mainly to see the ranch operations and learn about cattle production, so meeting this old farmer, who had been around for a while, seemed like a lucky break. Along with the beef information, he'd be able to get first hand information from someone who had experienced the ups and downs of family farms for many years.

"...Ya' know, life as an independent farmer or a rancher's never been easy," the farmer continued. "Many days, ya' rise before the sun wakes the rooster and work 'til the moon chases ya' inside for supper. Weather can be your best friend, waterin' your crops with just the right amount of water and warmin' them in the sun, or your worst enemy, drownin' your crops in angry downpours and bakin' them in a sun so hot ya' could fry eggs on the hood of yer tractor. I've lived through droughts, windstorms, floods, early freezes and late thaws. Most farmers do. But we tend to be a pretty stubborn bunch. Ya' might even hear some folks say that farmers live and die with each season. Every spring when we head out to the fields to plant our crops we hope for good weather so we can make enough money to keep farmin'. It's been that way for me and my family season after season after season. I guess it's pretty much like that for all the farmers I know too.

"Bill, other than the weather, what do you think is the biggest problem in farming today?" Martin asked.

"Well, we've always had problems of some kind or another. The Great Depression put a lot of good folks out of business, the Dust Bowls didn't help much either. I guess ya' could say that the American farmer's always struggled. And once the government started meddlin' with prices and givin' subsidies, things sure got turned upside down. We've had to deal with grain embargos, over-inflated prices, overproduction, wars, unfriendly interest rates, technology, and recessions. Every single one of those things, in one way or another, has given the independent farmer headaches over the years. But the biggest problem now, ya' ask? Especially for the independent farmer? Agribusiness. Corporate farmin'. There's just nothin' good about it. Those big farms sure've made a mess of things."

"How's that? How do corporate farms differ from what you and others like you do?" Martin asked.

"Well, there's lots to tell. But I doubt any of it'll really surprise ya'. Those big farms are owned by corporations that have deep pockets and stockholders to answer to. They don't have families to think about or back breakin' mortgage payments to make. They don't have to worry about havin' a bad year. Heck, if they have a bad year, they write it off and keep on movin'. We, small farms, well…we hope we'll be able to make the mortgage next month or pay the note on the new tractor we purchased in order to get our crops harvested. We've got debt collectors and our families to answer to. Corporations buy huge plots of land, bring in the latest 'quipment and set up their own processin' and packin' plants. Small family farmers, on the other hand, save for years to invest in any sort of upgrades. And we definitely can't afford to be processin' and packagin' our own goods. Shoot, we'd go broke before we broke ground for any kind of processin' plant. Also, most of us farm smaller plots of land so we can manage them properly. Factory farms don't care nothin' about the land or the animals they raise. To them, it all comes down to their bottom line. For us, it's a way of life and one we're pretty darn proud of. We feed the leaders of tomorrow and hungry folks all across the world."

"How much does agribusiness affect your ability to make money?"

"Well, between them and the government, it's a surprise any of us're still in business. Corporations produce truckloads of food which allows them to control the market and set low prices that don't allow us to break even. We don't have much control over them but they've sure got control over us. More and more these days, independent farmers're forced to sell their land, or they know the bank'll do it for them. We just can't compete. Our communities're fallin' apart. Lots of folks move to cities and suburbs to find jobs. A lot of small towns're emptyin' out. Shoot, Tommy and I've talked about sellin' a few times, but our natural meat production allows us to sell to specialized markets. It keeps us in business. We also grow organic hay for the winter and sell the excess to other natural beef farmers. It helps bring in a few extra dollars too. We'll be damned if we're goin' to give in."

"I appreciate all your insight into the life of a farmer, Mr. Newh...I mean Bill. Can you tell me a bit about cattle production, specifically antibiotic and hormone usage?"

"Well, hold yer horses for a second. Ye'r goin' to be interested in this other stuff first. Then I'll get to the cattle." Bill replied. "Time was, many years ago, there were close to seven million farms in the U.S. That's not the case anymore. Now there's just over two million. Unfortunately, only about twenty-five percent of the farms in operation today're family owned and operated and to top it off, every year we lose a few more. The other seventy-five percent're owned by corporations."

"I had no idea farming had changed so much."

"Yep, we small farmers suffer as corporations grow food and livestock usin' growth hormones, antibiotics, chemical fertilizers, herbicides, and pesticides. Most of that stuff ain't good for nothin' it comes in contact with, except for keepin' their precious bottom line low. Money's about the only thing they value. We're the ones who know the value of this land. We take great care to make sure our animals're treated right. We've got to work to make sure our soil remains fertile and our water remains clean. It's important to do what's right and work hard to build strong families and communities. We've got to keep doin' what we're doin'. It's in our blood. Sure, we've got tough competition but we ain't out of business yet, are we? We've got to keep makin' good, clean food for people and we've got to take care of this land."

Martin was impressed with how passionate the old farmer was about farming. "Bill, I cant' thank you enough for your time."

"Time's all I have anymore, son. But ya' can't leave until I tell ya' 'bout cattle production. I'm sure ya' need to get movin' along here pretty soon and I sure've been talkin' quite a bit, so I'll give ya' the short version. Stop me if you've got any questions." Martin nodded and the old farmer continued. "Most cows start life at a farm that specializes in bringin' cows to life. After a few months, they grow big enough to leave and get trucked to factory farms. And I use the term farm loosely. Those big, dirty plots of land aren't really farms at all. They're acres and acres of fields divided into pens. A company can keep tens of thousands of cows and monitor their growth to make sure that they can get'em to the market in 14 or 16 months. And the pens? They sure aren't out in the middle of beautiful green pastures where the cows get to roam and graze. They're just big dirt and mud feedlots where the cows get very little, if any, exercise. They sure aren't very sanitary places, either. When you put tens of thousands of cows into a confined area and pump them full of food, you've got a lot of waste to deal with. Most of the cows I've ever known don't know a thing about indoor plumbing." Bill chuckled and smiled. "Things get pretty messy. Most feedlots don't smell like rose gardens much either."

"I don't suppose they do," Martin laughed in response. "They sure don't sound like a place I'd want to stay too long at."

"I don't suppose many people do. Shoot, I don't suppose the cows like it much either. In fact, now that I've given ya' that delightful picture about the standard of livin' of cows, let me tell ya' a bit about how they're treated."

"I'm not sure I want to hear this."

"Ya' probably don't but ya' probably should." Bill replied. "Within a day or two of arrivin' at the farm, every cow gets injected with growth hormones. From that point on they're fed a diet consistin' mainly of cheap corn feed that has protein supplements and a regular course of antibiotics added. The antibiotics offset a variety of problems caused from the corn feed. It really ain't very good for the cows to eat corn. Corn feed can cause liver problems and makes stomachs bloat, but it's cheap and corporations like to keep their costs down. The unsanitary conditions don't help the health of the cows either, so why not give them antibiotics with every meal and offset everything. Did ya' know that most antibiotics in the U.S. are given to livestock? I don't remember the actual number, but it's somewhere around 70 percent."

"I didn't know that. That's pretty amazing, and pretty disturbing, especially with all the stuff we hear in the news these days about antibiotic usage being out of control."

"Yep, it sure doesn't sound too good to me. If one of my cows gets sick, I have to separate it from the rest of them. I can give it antibiotics if it needs it, but after that I can't sell it's meat as organic. My cows don't get sick much, though. The fresh air, the pastures, and the exercise keeps 'em pretty healthy. They're pretty hearty animals. Anyway, enough about my cows." Taking a deep breath, Bill continued. "Now, the growth hormone and protein supplements speed up the growth of each cow and add an extra 40 to 50 pounds per cow. Often times, the residues from the antibiotics and the hormones remain in the meat through the slaughterin' and packagin' process and end up in burgers and steaks all across the country. Not the type of thing that most folks know either, or the type of thing that Tommy and I want to be a part of."

"I can't imagine you would. In fact, I can't imagine anyone would."

"Well, I imagine most folks don't ever think too much about how farmers' decisions effect the food they eat."

So, how else do you run your farm differently?" Martin asked.

"Well, we haven't got thousands of cows. We don't use corn feed; our cows graze in the pastures on grass which is what they're meant to eat and when we need to, we feed 'em the hay that we grow in our fields. And like I said before, our cows move around and get exercise. Oh, and, they sure don't stand around in their own waste all day long. We don't inject 'em with hormones or add protein supplements or antibiotics to the feed. Overall, our cattle produce a much healthier type of meat – it contains those omega fatty acids folks're always goin' on about – because our cows eat what they're meant to eat. Unfortunately, regular folks who shop at the grocery store don't know much about us. We haven't got the marketin' power or the ability to produce the mass quantities of meat that factory farms do. And like I said, factory farm cows now make it to the market in a little over a year. It takes us quite a bit longer, maybe 2 to 3 years, to get our cattle ready for market. The deck's a bit stacked against us, wouldn't ya' say."

"It sure does appear that way. I hope things change sometime soon."

"We've been workin' to get things changed for awhile. Change takes time, but I think we're makin' progress. More folks're startin' to learn and're shoppin' at those organic food stores, but we've still got a long way to go. It'd sure be nice to see our little farm towns thrivin' again." Bill paused for a minute. "I know I've thrown a lot of information at ya' pretty quickly, do ya' have any questions?"

"You've given me a lot of things to think about, Bill. You've covered a lot of ground and answered more questions than I knew I had. I appreciate the time you've spent out here. It sure is nice looking out over the green hills and watching the clouds go by."

"This is one of my favorite spots in the whole world. I put this bench here many years ago. I sit on it just about every day."

"Would you mind if I called you if I have anymore questions?"

"Well, I don't do much 'round here anymore, so call anytime. And it sure gets borin' talkin' to Tommy and the cows!" Bill laughed.

"Well hopefully more cows'll have better things to say in the future. I hope you and your son continue farmin'. I'd hate to hear that you had to sell."

"Oh, we're not goin' anywhere," Bill assured him.

"Well, I'm afraid I'm going to have to leave. I have another appointment to catch. I'll have to take a pass on the tour of the place, but I'll try to swing back here another day to meet Tom and see the full operation. Meeting you and hearing you talk about farming has sure given me a lot to think about. And just for the record, Bill, there are those of us out there who do care about what you do. I'm hoping I can help to do something to spread the word."

"It'd sure be nice to have more people see things for how they really are. Thanks for takin' the time to visit our li'l piece of the country. Before you leave, let me run in and get ya' the names of those dairy farms."

"I'd forgotten about that. Good thing someone around here has a memory," Martin replied. "I sure do appreciate your time and I'll try to stop by again sometime."

Martin climbed into his car with new information and a few more numbers to call. His head spun. Who knew there was so much going on behind raising cattle? He had to do more research on the meat industry. Mr. Newhouse had really given him some insight. He didn't know how he would use the new information but he hoped one day it would come in handy.

꒰ ⑥ ꒱

Now, I don't want to go lettin' the darn'd cat out of the bag, but let me tell ya' this. That meetin' that Martin just had with our new friend Bill? Well, it'll have a big ol' impact on Martin's future. But for now, I'd better slow back down a bit and stay closer to the story at hand. I sure don't want to run out of story before I get to the all the good parts.

After the meetin' with the old farmer, all the pieces to the puzzle started fallin' into place for Martin. In fact, the picture came right into focus. Unfortunately, the picture wasn't too pretty and Martin didn't like it very much. Ya' see, the small farmers weren't organized. Sure, there were small co-ops scattered 'round the country but that was about it. There just wasn't anythin' on a national scale. How could there be? Farmers, after all, spent long days in the fields. They didn't have a whole lot of time left at the end of the day to go to meetins' for some pie in the sky idea that might or might not work. *"Ya' want every small farmer organized, you do it. I've got a farm to run and a family to feed,"* was more the attitude of the farmers. But I don't want ya' goin' off half-cocked thinkin' it's a negative attitude, 'cause it ain't. It's just reality. Granted, it's a tad bit short-sighted, but it's those farmer's reality for the most part, that's how they live. They work long hours and don't have much time to devote to other things.

Now, it's pretty lucky for them that Martin was new to all of this. Bein' an outsider probably helped because he didn't have any preconceived notions about how things're supposed to be done in the farmin' world. He didn't think outside the darn'd box, he lived outside of it, and he believed a national network of small family farms would solve a lot of problems. He believed an organization like that could sure make a real impact.

I guess ya' don't have to be a rocket scientist to figure out the direction Martin was headed. He figured with the right kind of attitude and the right kind of support, he'd get the resources together to help these folks out. A national farmin' organization, he thought, could band together and sustainable farmin' could regain some of the footholds it'd lost along the way. And when that happened, folks'd get better food to buy in the grocery stores and the land'd last a whole lot longer.

Chapter 7 ✿

Upon arriving home that afternoon, Martin's personal transformation started to take shape. In the weeks and months to come, he submerged himself in research. It's a wonder he didn't wear out his computer compiling file after file after file about natural beef farming and organic farming. On the phone, he spoke with people nationwide about their farming practices. He kept track of the types of organizations that helped them in the marketplace. He investigated organic food companies to see how they worked and learned about the growing market for organic food. Martin left no stone unturned. Eventually he would make so many contacts and learn so much about the industry that people would come to see him as a leader in the organics industry.

Once again, Martin had tapped into his creative side. In time, he would organize people, help others change the direction of their companies and help others devise new marketing strategies. No longer did he sit numbly behind a desk because the benefits and the schedule were good. As time moved on, however, and Martin became more active in the natural food industry, he wasn't satisfied. He felt like he wasn't doing enough. He hadn't yet been able to get farmers organized and he truly believed, once they did, it would revolutionize farming and in turn, change the food that people ate. It was this vision – the one where he saw healthy people everywhere eating healthy food, the one where the fast food industry felt choked off by neighborhood organic restaurants serving fresh, local produce and fresh local meats and dairy products – that kept him motivated and searching. He knew that if America was going to remain vital and productive that its farmers needed to be able to produce healthy foods for the masses. He knew that farmland needed to be looked after more carefully. He knew the chemicals had to go.

If ya' haven't figured it out yet, our friend Martin's embraced a cause. And, I might add, it's a cause we all need to be payin' attention to. It's a cause that has to do with every single one of us. After all, we live on this planet. We eat food. We all need to be payin' attention. Ya' see, this cause isn't just for us. It's for every-one who comes after us. It's a cause to save the earth by support-in' responsible, sustainable farmin' and if we don't all wake up and start payin' attention and maybe makin' a little ruckus when it's needed, the future looks pretty bleak.

Forgive me if I seem to be gettin' a tad bit carried away. I'll get down off my soapbox, now. Besides, the story demands that we come back to it and right around the corner, we'll be meetin' a couple more of those everyday, ordinary people I mentioned earlier. Ya' see, it just might turn out that Martin comes across a couple of folks who see things the way he does and thinks his cause is worth fightin' for. But, before I go and give the whole story away and ya' lose interest, I'd bet-ter move on. I've got a few more things to share with ya'.

Chapter 8

M artin needed help. If he was going to work to initiate changes in the agriculture and food industries, organize independent farmers, and help people see the value of healthier living, he had to have some assistance. He had found many people in the food industry who were already working in that direction, but the ones in agriculture were more difficult to find. Unfortunately, each time he found a lead, it seemed to fizzle out. Over the years, most farmers had become leery about outsiders who had made pie-in-the-sky promises. In response to the outsiders, they had learned to stick to what they knew and who they knew. And, Martin, of course, wasn't somebody they knew.

After coming up short time and time again, Martin reluctantly decided to focus his energies on the retail food industry even though he felt the change needed to start at the farm. Maybe, he thought, the change could happen backwards. Maybe if something happened in the food industry the farmers would be forced to respond. Martin, however, never really got a chance to get too involved on the retail side of the industry. Somehow he stumbled across a loose-knit farming group devoted to helping small family farms – the Independent Farmers Alliance's

(IFA). IFA's wanted to change the agricultural model and develop a plan that encouraged small farms to continue to use sustainable farming methods. They didn't, however, have enough resources to make a major impact. IFA needed someone who had the business know-how to develop and implement a successful plan. It wouldn't hurt if that person also had a well-developed network of contacts, either. And if that person also had strong belief in what they were trying to do, better yet.

Well, as it turns out, Martin had been looking for a group who wanted to make some changes but also who held the trust of farmers. IFA seemed like a perfect fit for him. Maybe he would finally be able to get something started. He knew if he was given a chance, he'd be able to get the job done. As soon as he heard about the group, he learned all that he could about them. He placed phone calls to the group and introduced himself. He learned about the types of projects they were involved in. Within a couple of weeks of making phone calls and sending emails, Martin discovered that IFA would be hosting its annual weekend retreat, a retreat they used to plan strategies for the upcoming year. When he inquired about it he was invited to attend.

As the plane departed from its gate and taxied to the runway, Martin's hopes were high. He wanted this short trip to be fruitful. He had already spent too much time following leads that turned into dead ends.

Upon arriving, Martin was relieved that the folks from IFA welcomed him openly. He felt like he belonged. During the opening evening, Nick Patterson gave the keynote address. Nick had also been invited for the weekend to facilitate one of the breakout sessions and to be the opening night speaker.

꒜ ⑥ ꒜

Now I know I'm not supposed to be interjectin' in the middle of the chapter, but I just can't help myself. Nick's one of those ordinary, everyday people I mentioned at the beginnin' of the story. We finally get to meet 'im. Remember, he's the one with the cowboy hat (and yes, he spoke to the group with his hat on) who has all of the experience workin' with ranchers and farmers. Of course, he and Martin've no idea how important they'll become to each other, but that's okay right now. They have to meet sometime, now, don't they?

꒜ ⑥ ꒜

Like most keynote addresses, the speaker always speaks a little too long, but in this case, Martin didn't seem to mind. Nick spoke a powerful message – one that sounded quite similar to the one that Martin had replayed in his head a few thousand times. Farming needed to change. Farmers needed to unite. Farmers have to continue to bring healthy food to the marketplace even if it takes more work. A growing market for healthy, clean food exists out there and farmers need to keep supplies going to it, etc, etc, etc. When Nick ended his address, the crowd gave him a warm applause. As he headed down from the podium, Martin was thrilled to see that Nick would be sitting at his table. He wasted no time introducing himself.

"Mr. Patterson, I'm Martin Trotter. Your message was timely. I couldn't agree with you more."

"Thanks Martin. I'm glad to know you. And please, call me

Nick. I'm only called Mr. Patterson by people who call my house trying to sell me something. I'm glad you liked the message. It's one I think we really need to focus our attention on this weekend. Hopefully we can make some inroads and come up with a plan. I'll be leading a breakout session tomorrow where we'll be discussing ways to organize farmers. You might want to come and check it out."

"Well, seeing as how that's what I'm looking to work on, I'd be glad to. Thanks for the information and the personal invite. Now, why don't you tell me how you got mixed up in this line of work."

The initial meeting between Nick and Martin got off on the right foot. The two men spent most of the evening getting to know each other and were excited to get started on the project the next day. Throughout their discussion, Martin admired the energy and passion Nick had in regards to family farms. He wanted family farms to flourish and was devoted to doing whatever he needed to do to help them get there. Martin felt that he had finally found someone who could help him in his cause.

As he retired to his hotel room for the night, Martin was re-energized. He held high hopes for the work that would be done the next day. He knew he could, with the help of Nick Patterson, create a plan for IFA that would make real progress towards promoting small family farms. He hoped they would be open to their ideas.

The next morning Nick led the breakout session and Martin, along with a handful of other folks, attended. As soon as the ideas began flowing, Martin and Nick clicked. Their collective energy and instant connection energized the rest of the group and together they created a plan that would promote a national brand of farm products from small, sustainable farms. The brand would promote the products using a marketing strategy that would educate the consumer about the differences between small farm practices and factory farm practices.

Later in the day, as the session came to a close, Martin, Nick, and the rest of the group headed back to the board meeting to present their plan. Nick would present the main plan and others in the group would add key points when they were needed. The group had drafted a solid plan and Martin finally felt like he was getting somewhere. He hoped, along with Nick and the rest of the group, that the IFA board would approve the plan and allow them to put it in motion.

As it turned out, the presentation went well. Nick's energy kept people interested and involved. Martin felt like they made progress. Unfortunately, it was only a feeling. The presentation would turn out to be the only thing that went well. When it came time for the board to decide on the proposal, they voted against it. After a pretty heated discussion and some boisterous complaints from the group, it became obvious to Martin that the board didn't have a concrete reason as to why. They just kept saying that it wouldn't work. Disappointed, Martin figured he knew what the real reason was. He had known going into this weekend that he would be considered an outsider – an outsider with a lot of vision and a lot of energy – but still an outsider, no less. His loyalty and worth had yet to be proven in the eyes of the IFA board. Maybe they just couldn't understand how an outsider could come in and help create a plan that they hadn't thought of themselves. Or, maybe the plan – a national plan – seemed too big for this group to manage. Or, maybe they just got hung up on the probable logistics that would go into starting a project with such great scope. But, for whatever reason, a good plan, maybe even a great plan, got shot down before it even had a chance to fail. In disgust, Martin left the retreat early. He'd wanted the weekend to be a success. Why couldn't this group see the possibilities? All he wanted to do was help! If people were going to have fresh, wholesome foods available to them at the market, sustainable farms had to remain in production and he had to find a way to help them do just that. He just needed to find the right organization and the right people.

ᔓ ⑥ ᔓ

Sometimes, it seems, we all get a little blind when it comes to change or big ideas. There always seems to be someone in the group who says ya' can't do this or ya' can't do that and then proceeds to give ya' a couple hundred questionable reasons why ya' can't. And, as good ol' human nature would have it, these folks always seem to be the vocal ones who tend to get everyone else's point of view all mixed up. Wouldn't it be nice, once in a while, if they all just backed off and let things happen? Wouldn't it? And so what if things headed south on occasion? It's just too darn bad people're afraid to take risks.

And other times? Well, in cases like the IFA board, it seems like folks might be a tad bit too comfortable with their own group to let others in. Luckily our boy Martin, even though he was pretty discouraged from the weekend's outcome, wasn't about to quit. No, he'd actually seen somethin' that re-inspired him. The group he'd worked with was chock full of people who wanted to see some changes made. And yes, they may've been the minority at the retreat, but they were there and they were willin'. Ya' sure've got to like that Martin'd found some more people who believed in his cause. Don't ya'? Besides, I don't think he was about to quit because one group didn't like the plan.

Chapter 9

A couple of months later, on a sunny afternoon, Martin sat in his office. He had looked over the rejected IFA plan several times since the retreat. The plan remained solid. He still couldn't understand why it had not been approved. The plan had great potential. *Oh well,* Martin thought. *Nothing can be done about it now. There's no sense in worrying about something that could've been. I've got to let this go and get back to what I was doing before this got in the way.* Martin was finally ready to put the retreat behind him. His consulting work and research had suffered a bit since the retreat. He had been unable to shake the frustration and disbelief from his experience at the IFA retreat. He had replayed the weekend over in his mind several times. Maybe he had overreacted a bit and left in too much of a hurry. There were, after all, people at the retreat who had believed as he did. There had been so much energy in the room when his group had created the plan. Maybe if he had stuck around a bit longer, he could have made more contacts and something good could have come out of the weekend after all.

At this point, however, he knew it was time to let bygones be bygones and refocus his attention towards things that he'd been neglecting and things that he could control. There was always more research to be done and new clients to be found to boost his lagging consulting work . In his spare time, Martin figured he could create a variety of plans that could be pitched to other agricultural groups around the country – plans that would work for farmers who grew vegetables and fruit, raised chickens, produced milk, etc. If he kept at it, he believed something else would surface soon. It had too.

And, it did. A few days later, after Martin began reinvesting himself in his work, the phone rang.

"Hello, this is Martin."

"Martin Trotter? This is Nick Patterson. We met a couple of months ago at the IFA retreat."

"Nick! It's good to hear from you. I've been kicking myself for not sticking around the retreat any longer. I've also been kicking myself for not getting your phone number. How are things in Colorado? Making any progress on your end?"

"Well, you didn't miss much after you left. A cloud of tension kind of hung over the rest of the weekend. I think the group might actually disintegrate. There were some pretty unhappy people who didn't like the lack of direction the board displayed."

"Well, that plan that we created had and still has a lot of potential. But that's old news. What's new with you? I'm surprised to get a call from you. I'm glad you tracked me down."

"You weren't difficult to find. I'm glad you're home. I've got something brewing that I think you might be interested in."

"I hope it's something good. I need something good. What've you got?"

"Well, I recently got a call from a colleague of mine regarding a grant through a large ranching cooperative that he thought I might be interested in. The grant would fund research to help family farms and ultimately lead to us creating some sort of business proposal for the group. We would specifically look at cows that are raised on a natural diet of grasses who aren't injected with growth hormones and fed antibiotics with each meal. If we develop something that seems plausible, it could mean revitalizing some rural communities. It would also promote healthier meat production. Did you know beef that comes from cows raised on grass is actually rich in the omega fatty acids that everyone is talking about these days? It's good for you."

"Actually, I heard that awhile back from an old farmer I spent some time with. I guess I should be eating more meat!" Martin continued. "But no, I haven't done much research on the cattle industry. You've piqued my interest. What else you got?"

"Not much, I just thought we might be able to incorporate some of our ideas from our proposal at the retreat."

"After I left the retreat, I looked that plan over several times. Boy would I love to continue working on something like that. I've been working on some other plans, on the side, that focus on different areas of food production, but I'd be willing to put all of that aside for now."

"That's what I was hoping I would hear from you. You've got the experience in the food industry and business expertise that I don't have. I know the cattle industry better than you do. I thought we'd make a good fit, especially after the way we worked together at the retreat."

"This sounds like something I can sink my teeth into. When do we start?"

"I'm flying to California in about a week for another farm conference north of Los Angeles. I can extend my trip a bit and head down to your neck of the woods so we can sit down and look over everything. How's your schedule look?"

"My schedule is officially cleared as of now. Is there anything you can send me before you arrive? I'd love to be able to look some things over before you get here."

"I'll drop some stuff in the mail today. And during our meeting next week, I figure we can split up the responsibilities and do the rest of the correspondence via email and fax machines. I'd like to try to limit the travel expenses if at all possible."

"Sounds great. Is there anything I should do to prepare for the meeting?"

"Other than bringing creative ideas with you, I can't think of anything. After working with you at the IFA retreat, I knew we needed to work together on something. I'm pretty excited about the possibilities."

"Well, I appreciate the call. I also appreciate that you thought of me. I'd been hoping the folks at the IFA retreat would be open to some of these ideas and I've been kicking myself for not getting contact information from everyone. I left that meeting pretty frustrated."

"You weren't the only one a little frustrated that weekend. This new project should get us back on track. It'll be good to work with you. I'll drop those things in the mail and see you next week. Call me if you have any questions."

"Will do. Thanks again."

Martin hung up the phone. He pushed himself away from his desk and leaned back in his chair. His thoughts were going a mile a minute. *Could this grant lead to something viable and productive? Could this guy be as committed to this cause as I am? Will we actually make progress and get some help to these family farmers?* He was cautious about getting his hopes up, but he couldn't help but feel like this might finally lead to some lasting change.

As Martin thought over the grant his excitement level grew. Nick, he had learned at the IFA retreat, had a great deal of experience working with farmers. He had been the president of the Granite Hills Farmers Union for several years. He had helped create nationwide standards for organic food production while he sat on the board of the Organic Foods Institute. He had also been involved with farm lobbyists and farm protests in Washington D.C. Nick understood the minds of ranchers and farmers, which was something Martin didn't quite have a handle on yet. In fact, Nick would help Martin understand a lot more about sustainable farming and farm production in the weeks and months to come.

৵ ⑥ ৵

Well folks, here we go. Martin and Nick're about to head down a path that'll lead 'em somewhere that even they can't predict. Along the way they'll pick up people who believe in what they're doin'. Ya' see, Martin and Nick're about to learn somethin' about workin' towards a cause. It's a lesson about folks just like you and me. Ya' see, if ya're confident in yer beliefs, if ya're passionate about yer cause, like-minded people will find ya'. When ya' believe in somethin' that helps people other people'll be drawn towards ya'. They'll be attracted to yer cause and yer desire to make things better. In many situations, it won't matter what ya' do as long as ya' work towards a greater good. Because, like I said before, most of us want to do the right thing. Most of us want to live in a better future and many of us won't mind helpin' out one little bit.

Chapter 10

After Nick and Martin's initial grant meeting, it didn't take long to realize that they had bitten off more than they could chew. They needed more brain power. Even with all of Martin's research and Nick's experience with farmers and ranchers, more research needed to be done. In order to come up with a solution for the farmers, they had to analyze the business operations of small family farms, specifically those that raised cattle. Questions needed to be answered. *How did these folks make a living when they were competing with corporate food giants? How could small farms become more competitive and more prominent in the marketplace? Exactly why is a smaller approach to beef production better? Is it better for the cows? Is it better for people?*

After weeks of questions being answered, the guys had to write a business proposal to the farmer's group in order to finalize the grant process. It was something neither of them felt real confident about doing. In fact, they were both starting to feel like the grant was much more than the two of them could handle. They were overwhelmed.

With all that Martin and Nick had to complete, frustration could have easily settled in. But it didn't. The guys realized there was a lot of work that stood before them but it didn't matter. They were working towards something bigger than them, something bigger than all of us. Besides, they had agreed at the beginning of the project that if help was needed they would find it. They weren't about to let their egos stand in the way of getting help to farmers. There was too much at stake and both of them deeply believed in the cause. For Nick, it was even a bit more personal. Having grown up around ranchers and farmers, he had seen the "For Sale" signs in front of the farms of families and friends who just couldn't keep it going any longer. And so yes, maybe they were coming at this project from different perspectives but they both knew that what they were doing could make a major impact.

One afternoon, after a morning of wading through research and trying to make some headway, Nick called Martin.

"Hey Martin, it's Nick."

"Nick, I was just about to call you. What's going on?"

"Well, I've been wading through all of this stuff and I can't seem to make any headway. I really think we need to find someone to help out. What do you think?"

"That's pretty funny. I was just about to call you and ask you the same thing."

"Well, I guess we agree we need help then," Nick replied.

"It appears that way. I've been thumbing through my Rolodex trying to find someone who might jump onboard with us. I can't seem to come up with anyone. Any ideas?"

"I've been doing the same thing. I'll place a few calls to people and let them know what we're up to and what we're looking for. Maybe something will come out of it. I sure was hoping you might have someone specific in mind. Don't you know everybody?"

"Not quite everyone," Martin laughed. "I wish I had someone in mind. It sure would make things easier. I'll do the same and put the word out through my industry contacts. Normally, I hear a lot of stuff, but I haven't heard of anyone looking for anything recently. I guess I'll just keep trying. How's your research coming?"

"Well, the research is coming along great. But I still can't come up with an idea to pitch to the rancher's group. Maybe when we meet in a couple of weeks I'll have something. Either way, I'll create some sort of a summary of the research I've done and send it to you. Maybe you'll see something that I haven't. There's quite a bit of information to share, so I'll send it to you in increments. I imagine it's going to open your eyes and make this whole thing seem that much more important."

"I'm interested in what you've found. I haven't come up with any ideas either. Maybe this'll help. I'll send you what I have so far also."

"Sounds great. By the way, the stuff I'm sending is about cows and farms."

"Gee, thanks," Martin laughed. "I'm looking forward to learning more. In the meantime, let me know if anyone comes pounding on your door. We sure can use the help."

"I'll do that. See you at the next meeting."

As it turns out, the networking that Martin and Nick are about to do will actually work rather quickly. Fortunately for the guys, Mark McClure, is between jobs. One morning, about a week after Nick and Martin had talked, Mark received a phone call from a past associate telling him about a group that needed help on a grant that would help small family cattle producers. Mark, having spent some time working in the dairy industry and seeing all of the problems associated with modern day milk production, thought this might be something he should look into. His associate had left him Martin's number so he picked up the phone and dialed the number.

"Hello Mr. Trotter? My name is Mark McClure."

"Mark McClure? Your name sounds familiar, but I don't know that I've met you. What can I do for you?"

"Well, I heard that you're working on a grant that deals with cattle production. I got a call from a past associate of mine who said you guys were looking to bring someone in to help. I'd like to know more. I'm very much interested in what you're doing even though I know very little about it."

"Mark McClure. Weren't you responsible for getting Sunshine organic dairy into the large grocery stores?"

"Yep, that's me. I haven't been with Sunshine for a little while though. It was time for me to do something else. I'm still interested in working in the organic food industry, though. I still believe there are a lot of people out there who would buy organic if they only knew more about it. It wouldn't hurt if it were a little less pricey, too."

"Well, it sounds like you might be the guy we're looking for. Let me tell you a bit about our project and we'll see what you think."

Martin and Mark spent the next half an hour discussing the details to the grant and learning about each other. Martin definitely liked what he heard on the other end of the line – an experienced corporate exec between jobs looking to make an impact somehow. This guy sounded too good to be true.

"My partner, Nick Patterson, and I are meeting next week for our monthly update meeting. Sometimes we meet in my neck of the woods here in California. Sometimes we meet in Colorado, the place that Nick calls home. Next week we'll be in Colorado. Is there any possibility that you can meet us?"

"It should be a short drive for me. I live in the Denver area. I'd love to meet with you and see if this is something I can help you guys with. What you've told me so far sounds great. The grant sounds great, the work that you're doing sounds great, everything. I look forward to meeting you."

"Likewise. Why don't you give me your email address and..."

While Martin and Mark worked out the details for next week's meeting, Martin had already decided to surprise Nick and just bring Mark along. A pleasant surprise would help ease the stress they were both feeling and Martin had a good feeling about Mark.

ॐ ⑥ ॐ

Have ya' ever worked on a project that just seems like it's the best darn thing in the whole world? Ya' know, one of those projects that absorbs yer attention from the time ya' wake up in the mornin' 'til ya' go to bed at night. And to top it off, ya' dream about it? That's how this project'd become for both Nick and Martin. Whenever a spare moment popped up, the grant and natural beef farmin' controlled their thoughts. Over pancakes and sausage, they thought about the grant. When they were drivin' down the highway, they were thinkin' about cows. Instead of countin' sheep at night, they counted cows. And what they were thinkin' wasn't small potatoes. No, they were thinkin' big. Martin'd been energized by Nick's passion about the grant and his passion for farmin'. Nick'd been energized by Martin's unwaverin' belief in the fact that they could turn this into somethin' big and help out many folks. And now, they'd gotten a new ally. Someone new'd arrived on the scene, someone they couldn't have foreseen, and he showed up at a time when they really needed him.

Chapter 11

The following week, Martin showed up to breakfast in his flip-flops and shorts – not quite mountain wear, but he was comfortable and it was summertime in Colorado. He and Nick always met at the same little mom and pop diner to kick off their meetings. It lacked the tension of a meeting room and allowed them to feel more at home, besides, the food was all homemade. And since they always took good care of the waitresses, no one ever complained that they sat at their booth too long. Not long after Martin sat down, Mark, an outdoor enthusiast, showed up looking like he was ready to go for a hike. Hanging off of his shoulder was the same beat up backpack that he had carried for years. Mark had never gotten used to carrying a briefcase, even as the head of Sunshine, and he apparently wasn't about to change his habits now. For a guy who liked things neat and orderly, the backpack seemed out of place. He introduced himself and sat down across from Martin. After a few minutes, Nick, who always arrived a few minutes late, showed up in jeans and his trusty cowboy hat. Anyone looking at the three of them never would have guessed that they were meeting on business.

As Nick walked up, he looked at Martin with one of those, "Who the heck is sitting in my seat?" looks on his face. Martin smiled, stood up and introduced Nick and Mark.

"Nick, I'd like you to meet Mark McClure. Mark's here to meet with us today to learn about our grant and decide whether or not he might like to come on board."

"Nice to meet you Mark. Apparently, you've just learned a bit about Martin. He likes to keep people in the dark a little from time to time. I'm sure he spoke with you before today. Funny, but he didn't mention it. It must have slipped his mind." Martin smiled.

"Glad to meet you also Nick." Mark replied. "I hope this isn't…"

"Oh, of course not. Martin just loves to mess around sometimes. He likes the surprised looks he gets from people. It's just one of his things. No, I'm sure if you're here, you must have some solid credentials. Martin's standards are high and he's not one to waste his own time."

"Mark called me last week…" As Martin explained everything, the three gentleman sipped their coffee and ordered their breakfast. Martin's little prank had broken the ice nicely and everyone warmed into the day. After breakfast had been served, eaten, cleared away, and hot coffees refilled, the guys got down to business.

Martin explained about the grant. He spoke glowingly about Nick and all of Nick's experience. He explained how excited they were to be working on something that might actually have a lasting impact in the field of agriculture. He also explained where he saw Mark fitting in.

"…so as part of the grant process, we have to write a business proposal. The proposal must show the ranchers' co-op how we can implement our ideas. We need someone like you, someone who is good with details and specifics, someone who knows a heck of a lot about creating a company from the ground up, to help us with the plan. We also need someone who knows natural foods. We need someone who believes in natural and organic foods and after speaking with you and looking over your experience, I can't think of a better person than you, Mark. We really need your help."

"Well, Martin, as you know from our discussion last week, I recently left my position at Sunshine so this seems to be coming at the right time for me. Your project sounds like it could have a significant impact on the natural farming scene, similar to the impact we had with organic milk. Let me think it over, talk with my wife about it some more, and I'll let you know before you leave town."

"Sounds great Mark. We look forward to your call. Even if you haven't made a decision before I leave, you can always meet up with Nick. You both live in the area."

"And Mark, just so that you know, I think we'd be lucky to get you in on this. You have the experience we need and I'm pretty sure that we could all work together. It was nice to spend some time with you this morning. I hope it won't be the last." Nick said.

Martin and Nick spent the rest of their day back at Nick's going over the grant, constantly bringing up Mark and what he could offer them. Throughout the conversation, Martin couldn't help but think that the pieces seemed to be falling into place. He was almost certain Mark would call back and accept their offer. He thought he could hear it in his voice and read it in his body language. He also knew that Mark was interested in creating real change in food production. He was a staunch proponent of organics and believed everybody was entitled to healthy, naturally grown food.

By nightfall, the two men were ready to talk about anything that didn't relate to beef. They were also ready to head for dinner. On the drive to the restaurant, Martin's cell phone rang. He could see on the caller i.d. screen that it was Mark.

"Hey Mark. You're calling back soon, which means either you're ready to jump in with both feet or there's absolutely no way you can devote your time and energy to this project right now. I'm hoping, however, that it's my first prediction."

"I've thought about calling you back since the moment I drove away from the diner. I can't wait to get started. I spoke with Carol about it and she's all for it. She knows how much I care about organic foods. She also knows I've been looking for a project like this. When do I start? What do I do?"

"Well, if you can get away for dinner tonight, we'd be glad to have you meet us. Heck, bring Carol and the family if you'd like. Nick's treat." Martin said with a wink over at Nick. "But seriously, come on out this evening if you can. We won't talk shop, we promise. If that doesn't work, meet us tomorrow morning at the same diner. We'll get you a copy of the grant, a copy of our ideas so far, and a copy of the format of everything. We also have a synopsis of all of the research that we've done so you can get an idea of what we're thinking about. How's that sound?"

"Sounds like a plan. I have to say, Martin, this is coming at a good time for me. I've been looking for something to devote my attention to. I have to thank you for believing in me. It's a great compliment. Thanks."

"Ever since you called, I've been hoping you'd join us. We're glad to have you working with us. Now, are you going to meet us for dinner or not?"

"It would be my pleasure."

Touchdown! Martin got off the phone elated. He hadn't expected a reply quite that soon, but it was a relief to know they had someone strong who could really help them with their proposal. He couldn't wait until the morning's meeting so they could get Mark caught up and thoroughly immersed in the project.

So here's the thing. It don't do ya' no good to believe in somethin' and keep it to yerself. It also don't do ya' no good to not ask for help when ya' need it. Martin and Nick're pretty smart guys and they knew that the grant couldn't be written well with just the two of 'em. There's simply too much to do. The cause, after all, was just too darn big. Besides, they knew the project'd benefit from some fresh thinkin' so why not make a few calls. It sure couldn't hurt none. Anyways, as a general rule, when ya' put the word out and others pass it along, nine times out of ten, someone, and usually someone who has similar values and interests, shows up. The fancy term for doin' this is called networkin' but I just call it openin' the phone book.

In our story's case, Mark showed up. Mark needed the guys just as much as they needed him. It was a perfect fit. Now, this won't be the last time this happens in our story, but since Mark was our first, I thought we'd stop a minute to discuss it. Ya' see, most folks're willing to help out with things they believe in when given the opportunity. Often times, however, it's not about the desire of folks to get involved, it's just that they don't know they're needed, which is why, especially in this case, networkin' plays an important role.

Chapter 12 ⑥

A month or so, after Mark came onboard, the group came together for one of their regular monthly meetings. The research had been easy. The biggest problem they faced now was trying to figure out how to help the ranchers turn more of a profit. They had run through several ideas, sending email after email to each other, but no idea seemed feasible or practical or both. They knew, however, that once they figured it out, the business plan would come together nicely. In the month or so since they last met, Martin had been pushing himself pretty hard to come up with ideas. Mark had started to wonder whether they'd ever find something that they could run with. And Nick? Well, after a couple of weeks of frustrating email correspondence, Nick decided to take a step back for a few days. He felt like he was too close to everything, so he fueled up his little Cessna, loaded up his fishing gear and flew to one of his favorite, secluded lakes for a quiet week of fly fishing and cricket talk. By the time he returned, he felt refreshed and ready to find a solution. In fact, on his flight back home, he remembered a piece of research that he'd come across a while back. It sparked an idea that he decided to keep to himself until they met in a few days. He hoped it would give the guys some hope and give the group something to feed off of.

On the morning of the meeting, Martin and Mark showed up a few minutes early. They wanted to get things going. Little did they know, but things would definitely get going when Nick arrived.

When Nick arrived at the diner, a little bit late as always, he carried a small cooler and had one of those agitated looks on his face. His forehead was wrinkled, his hands wouldn't stop moving, and he couldn't stand still. As he sat down to order breakfast, he didn't give Martin or Mark a chance to start talking. He jumped right in. He'd held onto his idea long enough.

"Alright. I know we usually catch everybody up on their progress before we get started. I know I'm jumping the gun here, but if I don't get this information out to you guys, I might explode."

"That would be messy," Martin chuckled. "We definitely don't want to have to clean your body parts off the floor, so please, before I'm picking your heart off the floor, give us what you've got. By the way, what's in the cooler?"

"Huh? Oh, yeah. The cooler. I caught some lake trout last week and thought Mark might like to take some home with him. In fact, if you guys don't have plans for dinner tonight, I thought I'd have you over and grill some trout using my secret recipe. Anyway, here Mark. It's frozen and packed pretty well in ice. It should be fine until you get home."

"I love trout. Thanks Nick. Now, what's this about fishing? You've been off fishing while we've been scouring the internet for ideas? I see, leaving the new guy to do all of the work, eh?" Mark joked.

"Here's the deal, I was about ready to slaughter myself at the local beef yard if I didn't get away. Anyway, the trip did what it was supposed to do. I don't really know where to start, so I'll just jump in somewhere. As I flew back home, I remembered some research I'd done a while back. It sparked an idea. I'm thinking some of this information will help us come up with a real plan of attack. Okay, here it goes." Nick took a sip of coffee and began. "It's no wonder these family farms struggle so much. Sometimes they have to pay to have their excess cattle carcasses removed. Stuff that makes the big factory farms and processing plants a profit."

"Whoa there, big fella. Nick, you're losing us. Take a couple of steps back and start from the beginning," Martin said.

"Okay. You're right. I've just got all of this information swimming around in my head. Check this out. Nick passed a couple of papers towards the guys. "This diagram shows what happens to a cow after it goes to the slaughterhouse to be turned into food. Take a look. Natural meat farmers get a premium price for their steaks and tenderloins. In fact, they have no problems selling their high quality prime cuts of meat. Consumers like to know that they're buying high quality, fresh, natural meat and don't mind paying a bit more for it. It's tasty and it it's chemical free. I mean, who doesn't like a prime cut of meat? Steak and roast sales are the best part of the deal for these farmers. Unfortunately, after all the good stuff is sold, it all goes downhill quickly. Shoot, it's too bad the entire cow isn't made up of prime cuts. We'd be looking for something else to spend our time on. Anyway, if you look back at the chart, you can see that the farmer also sells the lean grind – the stuff they make burgers and sausages out of – but when it's all said and done, the prime cuts and the lean grind only make up 28% of the cow leaving the farmer with a whole bunch of cow and nothing to do with it."

"You mean to tell us that we only eat about 28% of the cow?" Mark asked.

"Yep. After the farmer has sold off the good parts of the cow, he's left with a little over 70% of the carcass. Of course a lot of the carcass is bones, but there is still some usable stuff left."

"Why doesn't he sell the other usable stuff?" Mark asked.

"Well, he can't compete because the factory farms create so much scrap meat that they can sell it for next to nothing."

"Sounds like a problem. What else happens in general in the meat industry?" Martin asked.

"Well, in general, the meat industry is controlled by factory farms, or concentrated animal feeding operations (CAFOs). In fact, they aren't farms in the traditional sense. The conditions are horrible. Imagine hundreds of acres of grassless land, dried dirt or mud depending on the time of year, fences formed into hundreds of pens, and tens of thousands of cows walking around in each other's waste. These huge feedlots keep animals penned together in groups and each group is fed an unnatural diet made mostly from corn that is chock full of protein supplements and antibiotics designed to fatten up a cow as quickly as possible in order to get it to the market. Anyway, I'm getting off topic. I just hate what these CAFOs do with the cattle. It's inhumane. Most people would stop eating beef if they ever visited one of these places. How they've managed to get us all to believe that the cows we eat are all out frolicking in the countryside, is beyond me. People need to wake up. And to top it off, corn fed beef isn't nearly as good for people as grassfed beef. Anyways, I'm way off topic. Let me go back in the direction I was headed."

"So, other than the conditions and the quantities of cows, how do these factory farms work differently?" asked Mark.

"Well, the biggest thing that happens is that they produce a lot of cows quickly which means they have a lot of cows to sell. Because they have so many cows to sell and they feed them such a cheap diet, they control the market. After a cow is slaughtered and processed, all its leftovers, the stuff that isn't usable, gets sold to rendering plants where everything gets turned into 'beef meal' which is then sold for a variety of different purposes. Because the CAFOs create so many leftovers, they can sell it for a much cheaper price and still make a profit. The family farmer, on the other hand, barely breaks even selling the steaks and the lean grind. When it comes to the leftover meat, they usually take a loss. In fact, sometimes the small farmer even has to pay someone to take the stuff away. It's actually kind of sad. Here we have farmers who treat their cattle humanely, feed them a diet of natural grasses, and let them roam in pastures, and yet, these poor guys can't catch a break. They try to do the right thing but the CAFOs force them out of business."

"Okay, I think we get the picture, but I don't think we have a clue as to where this is going. What is all this getting to Nick? When you got started, you sounded like you had some sort of an idea." Martin said.

"Well," Nick answered, "In terms of our business proposal, we can't do anything about the prime cuts and lean grind. Those take care of themselves. The leftovers – the trim, the livers, and the hearts – all have a market, but the natural meat farmer is priced out of this market. So, here's where I'm heading with this. Since the leftovers are usable and natural meat farmers can't sell them anywhere, we need to find an outlet for them. I think that's what we really need to look at. We need to find a place where they can sell this stuff and turn a profit?"

"Any ideas where they can sell this stuff?", Mark asked.

"Well, I don't really know yet, but I think it's the breakthrough we've been looking for. I thought each one of us could look into some possibilities for our next meeting. I think it's going to be the key to this. If we can find a market, it'll really help these farmers out. They'll be able to sell more of their cows and bring in more money," Nick replied.

"You know, I think you've helped us turn a corner," Martin said. "After we eat and catch up, why don't each of us tap into some resources and see what we can find. In the meantime, if any light bulbs go on, let us all know. If we can come up with some good ideas, they might turn out to be the key to our business proposal. This stuff is great. Thanks for doing all this, Nick." Martin said. "Oh, and by the way, I'll be over for the secret grilled trout. What about you, Mark?"

"Oh, I wouldn't miss it. In fact, maybe Carol can steal this secret recipe and make it for me when we thaw out the trout in this cooler."

"Hey now, it's a secret for a reason," Nick replied.

"I hope it's not a secret because it's so bad," Martin joked. "Shall I bring some backup takeout?"

Martin, Mark, and Nick spent the next couple of days coming up with leads and losing them. They made lists, they gathered information, they discussed, and although they didn't end up with anything substantial, when they all departed, they felt as if they were on to something. Finding a market for this stuff sounded like it was going to be the key, the key to a strong business proposal and ultimately the key to helping out farmers who struggled to run their farms in a sustainable, environmentally friendly manner.

Sometimes ya' just can't force ideas. Sometimes, like a farmer tendin' to his fields, ya' have to turn over the soil, plant the seeds, add some water, and wait for somethin' to grow. In our case, the guys'd already turned over a lot of soil. The research they'd compiled just about qualified them as experts. Unfortunately, they found somethin' promisin' and tried too hard to nurture it. Many times they overwatered it or weren't patient enough with it, and, as anyone who's ever grown anythin'll tell ya', plants need a little attention and a lot of patience. I guess ideas're a lot like that, sometimes too. We spend too much time fiddlin' with 'em instead of steppin' back, lettin' the sunshine do its work and waitin' for the ideas to grow. It's good, after all, to plant a garden and leave it be a little bit. If you keep fussin' with it, nothin's ever goin' to grow. Our boy Nick seems to be the only one who remembered that, but then, Nick's also the only one in the group who has much experience in the farm world. It's a good thing he had the foresight to take a few steps back. It did wonders for Martin and Mark. It'll also do wonders for the project and the cause.

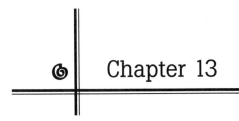

Chapter 13

Soon, the leaves on the trees began to turn and along with the reds and the oranges came discouragement. A couple of months had passed, beef industry research flowed from everyone's ears, and no one had been able to take Nick's idea any further. Searching for a solid idea had become more work than any of them had imagined. A couple of times they felt like they were close, but when they started to create the business plan, things fizzled. They had been bouncing ideas around through email but none of them seemed inspirational. They just couldn't seem to find the right path to take. They knew they were in the right forest, but somehow they kept returning to the same spot.

As they reconvened for a monthly meeting, Nick was surprised when he reached the diner and Martin and Mark weren't there yet. When Martin arrived a couple of minutes later, he seemed to walk with a little less bounce in his step. A quiet, somber air seemed to surround both of them. As they headed into the diner, Mark pulled up. As he stepped out of his pickup, all Martin and Nick could see was a huge smile.

"What's with him?" Nick asked.

"You've got me, but I hope it's good news," Martin replied.

"Boy, you guys look as if your world is coming to an end and I'm not so sure I want to set foot in it right now. Is it safe?" Mark teased.

"I suppose you've shown up with your superhero cape on ready to save the day," Nick said.

"Well, actually, my cape is at the cleaners, so I've come in Clark Kent mode. It's time for some action. But this superhero is hungry. Why don't we go inside, sit down, order some food and then get onto saving the world."

"Yeah, I am pretty hungry," Martin replied. "But I'm not going into that diner until you settle down a little bit. You're making me nervous."

The waitress had their table all ready for them when they entered. She had seen them in the parking lot and made sure their regular table had three steaming cups of coffee waiting. As the guys slid into their booth, Mark started up again.

"Hey Martin, you have dogs, don't you?"

"Yeah, our shepherds are part of the family. Why do you ask?"

"Have you ever seen Dr. Ball on any of the syndicated talk shows?" Mark asked with the grin still smeared across his face.

"Yeah, I've seen Dr. Ball. Why do you ask?" Martin replied.

"Wait a second. Who's Dr. Ball?" Nick asked.

"She's that medical doctor who doesn't act like a medical doctor. She's written some books about preventative healthcare instead of prescriptive healthcare. She approaches medicine from a different angle. She thinks people would be a lot more healthy if they ate fresh foods and exercised regularly. She treats her patients with diet, exercise, and dietary supplements before she ever prescribes drugs. It drives the other medical doctors crazy," Martin replied. "She's outspoken but she makes a lot of sense. The drug companies don't like her much either."

"She sounds like a chiropractor I know," Nick replied.

"Yeah, she kind of acts like it but since she's an M.D. who graduated from a prestigious Ivy League medical school, she's not written off as a quack," Martin said.

"Sounds like a doctor I might like to meet," Nick replied. "So, what's this Dr. Ball have to do with us?"

"Well," Mark began. "I guess she's a dog person too. The other day I caught her on a talk show complaining that she couldn't find many options for feeding her Golden Retrievers natural dog food. I guess when one of her dogs became seriously ill, she did a bit of research on dog food. It turns out that many of the dog food products that claim to be "natural" contain animal by-products and slaughterhouse scraps."

"Well this sure is a nice discussion to start off our breakfast with. Do I want to hear this? Sometimes it's good to be ignorant isn't it? Do I really want to know what's in my dog's food? Do I really need to know?" Martin asked.

"Well, you might. I have the beginnings of an idea. In that same show, Dr. Ball stated how disgusted she was with her discovery and that she'd been trying to find a product that was better for her dogs. When the host on the show mentioned the various types of vegetable-based dog foods, the doctor said she had considered them, but, dogs are carnivores. She wanted to feed them natural food that imitated what might be eaten in the wild, but, she didn't want to have to prepare raw meat for them each day. She sounded pretty determined."

"But what does that have to do with us?" Nick asked.

"Dr. Ball wants natural dog food. We have a natural beef source. Why couldn't we take the leftovers – the trim, the hearts and the liver – and use them as the protein base for a truly all natural dog food?" Mark replied.

"Dog food? You want the ranchers to make dog food? They don't know anything about making dog food. Shoot, they feed their ranch dogs whatever's available at the feed store. I can't see them wanting to make dog food." Nick replied.

"Hold on a minute, Nick. Mark might be on to something. I think it's a pretty interesting idea. Let's not throw it out the window before we get a chance to look at it. Besides, you and I don't seem to be fountains of ideas lately," Martin said. "In fact, as this idea runs over in my head, it's starting to make sense. I'd be willing to buy an all natural dog food. Our dogs are part of our family. You should see how my wife spoils them. We already buy premium food for them because we assume it's a healthier choice. I'd buy something even better for them," Martin added.

"Do you think it's feasible, Mark? You've got more production and marketing experience than I have. I'm just the farm guy, remember. Have you put much thought into this?" asked Nick.

"Actually, I can't get the idea out of my head," Mark continued. "Ever since I saw Dr. Ball speak, I can't stop thinking about it. I definitely think we should look into it. I've only had time to look into it a little bit, but there aren't really many choices out there for folks who want to feed their pets good, all natural food. There are some small, niche, regional brands, but nothing nationwide. And you guys know that there are a lot of people out there like Martin who feel that their pets are part of their family. They go to great lengths to make sure their pets are well cared for."

"You make a pretty good point, Mark. Our family would be lost without our dogs too," Nick said. "You know, this might be the idea we've been looking for. Sorry I jumped on you so quickly. Dog food just seemed like such a weird idea at first. So, since you've been running this idea around in your head, do you have any suggestions?"

"There's my problem. That's why this is the beginning of an idea. I've thought about a lot of stuff and I think the pet food idea is sound, but I don't know where to go from here. Besides, I wanted to run it by you guys before I did too much," Mark said.

"It sounds like we all might need to look at some pet food companies and pet food production," Nick stated.

"I have some experience in the pet food industry, but it was a long time ago," Martin said. "There are probably a few people I can call from back then, but I sure don't remember much."

"I think this gives us something to focus on," Nick said. "It sounds like an idea with a lot of potential and promise. I say we throw all of our attention towards this pet food thing and see what we come up with. Sound like a good idea to everyone?" The group all nodded their heads in agreement as Nick finished his question. "Great then. Let's see what we can come up with."

By the time pancakes, eggs, and bacon had been brought to their table, the somber mood had lifted. Energy flowed during their discussions. The possibilities seemed to grow as they spent the rest of the day bouncing ideas around and calling possible contacts. None of them could believe they had arrived at an idea that had to do with pet food. Who would have thought that their research into natural meat production would lead them towards pet food? Not steaks, not pot roasts, not even hamburgers. Pet food. They were going to be looking at food for canine consumption, not human consumption. When they started this project, if you had asked any of them if they thought that their research would lead them to pet food, they would have laughed.

꙳ ⑥ ꙳

Of course I knew that our boys were goin' to get to this pet food idea, but it still makes me scratch my head every time I think about it. When it comes down to it, I guess most of us don't consider what we feed our pets. Maybe if we paid just a little more attention to them we might actually learn a little bit. Who knows what ya' might learn from a dog or a cat? Heck, who knows what ya' might learn at any given time? Take a look at Mark. He'd been sittin' at home in his recliner, pokin' the buttons on his remote control just tryin' to relax. He wasn't really lookin' for an inspirational idea at the time. But here's the thing. Inspiration often comes at times when ya' aren't lookin' for it, so when it comes, ya've got to be ready for it like Mark was. And sometimes, what might seem inspirational might also seem a bit crazy. I mean, none of our guys'd even considered makin' dog food. Shoot, don't ya' remember how Nick reacted at first? He thought Mark'd gone off his rocker. Thank goodness he'd had enough sense to listen to him.

I believe life'd be pretty borin' if it weren't for folks who chased crazy ideas and saw 'em grow into somethin'? Sometimes it just pays to be open to new ideas. I know it sounds like some sort of old cliché but it really is true. The world might be a little bit better place if we were all a bit more open. Heck, maybe this story might even turn into somethin' inspirational for ya' if ya' hang around long enough to see it through to the end.

Chapter 14

Heading off with pet food on their minds, the guys were determined to turn Mark's idea into something. At the next meeting, they would need to start putting the presentation together. In the meantime, they'd each work on their separate tasks and report back to each other. They were all aware of the pressure to make this new pet food idea work and it finally felt good to have a goal in mind.

Back at home, as the guys started looking into pet food, they began sharing information via email.

Hey guys.
Check this out. Did you know that one out of every three households in the U.S. has a pet? Also, pet food sales alone bring in around $14 billion dollars a year. There's got to be a market for a truly natural pet food. A natural pet food brand has the potential to be successful. There's definitely a growing market for natural organic human foods. I bet we can tap into that same consumer base in terms of being able to sell pet food. If any of you frequent any natural food or organic food stores, check their pet sections and see what they offer. I'll keep sending out info as I find it. You guys do the same.—MT

Martin and Mark,

I've got something that might help us market this stuff? Ever take a moment to look at the label on your dog or cat food bags? Rendered proteins, often listed as chicken meal, meat meal, beef meal or beef by-products make up the protein source found in most pet foods. Even a few pet foods that claim to be 'all natural' use rendered proteins. The rendering process, without going into too much gory detail, is basically a boiling process. The other half of the cow, chicken, or pig that isn't consumable goes to rendering plants. Bones, spinal tissue, brain tissue, a variety of slaughterhouse scraps, etc. all find their way into giant vats where they are boiled down. The dried up stuff becomes the "meal". Rendering plants are the redheaded stepchild of the meat processing industry. It tries to keep them out of the public eye as much as possible. They don't deny their existence, they just ignore them. Besides, how many people really want to know what ends up in those vats?

So, now that I've given you some images you probably didn't care to have running around in your head, there's got to be a way we can use this to our advantage. How many people want their dogs and cats eating protein that comes from questionable sources?"

We've got to be able to use this as part of a marketing strategy when it comes to having a truly all natural dog food.

—Nick

About a week after Nick's email, Martin's phone rang in his office. Being in the middle of a project, he decided to let the answering machine pick it up.

"Martin, this is Nick. Hey listen. You're not gonna believe this. I've got an idea that I think we can write into the plan. We all need to meet as soon as..."

"Hello Nick. Hey, it's Martin. Sorry, I'm in the middle of a project. What's all this about?"

"I think I've got it. I think I've got the pet food plan. I've been so fired up and grossed out about the rendering plants that I haven't been able to do anything other than try to come up with an idea to get this thing going. I think I've got the plan now. Do you know about Jerry's Bakery?"

"No, but I think you just came up with a great marketing slogan. How does, 'Saving the Earth, one bag of dog food at a time' sound? Has a nice ring to it, don't you think?"

"Funny, Martin. What? Are we watching cartoons on Saturday mornings now? Are you going to call in the Justice League to help out? I hear Spider-Man's available. He's between movies at the moment. Now, can I get you to concentrate? Can you stay with me for just a minute?"

"Oh, alright. What's this about a bakery?"

"I can't believe I haven't thought of this before. Jerry's Bakery is owned by the Grain Belt Farmer's Cooperative."

"Okay, what does that mean for us?"

"Well, the cooperative is made up of a couple of hundred wheat farmers who were sick and tired of making next to nothing on their wheat. So, they raised about 5 million dollars and bought a bakery and a grain mill. They supply the wheat for the breads they make. They've become quite successful and their breads are now trucked all across the country. Some of their customers are large chain restaurants. It's a pretty amazing success story."

"I'm glad you aren't telling me that wheat farmers have decided to market a 'whole wheat' dog food. They could boast about the fiber content! I wouldn't want to compete with that." Martin joked. "And I don't see how this applies to us, Nick, we can't bake cow bread." Martin heard a few chuckles on the other end of the line.

"I know we can't bake cow bread, Martin, although my mom's meatloaf is pretty good. But, what we can do is model our proposal after their bakery. We can recommend to the farmers group that they create a pet food company – one that they supply the meat to and one that sells its product straight to the grocery stores. I think it'll work."

"They're farmers and ranchers, Nick. They aren't factory owners and pet food distributors."

"I know, I know. But, if the wheat farmers can do it, I don't see why the meat farmers can't borrow a page from their book."

"Well, you might be right. Since other farmers have been successful at it, maybe they'd be willing to take a look at it."

"I think so. We all need to sit down and hash this stuff out as soon as possible. We are, after all, running out of time. We're supposed to meet three weeks from now. Can we meet tomorrow? Or Thursday?"

"I'll free up my schedule. I can probably catch a flight tomorrow or Thursday. Why don't you call Mark and tell him what's going on. If he's busy, the two of us can meet. I'll book a flight as soon as I hang up. This is great stuff, Nick. Great stuff. I'm getting excited."

"Yeah, me too. I can't stop thinking about it." Nick replied. "Once you've booked your flight, let me know when you'll be getting in."

As soon as Martin hung up the phone, Nick was on the phone to Mark. Mark would be able to meet. He hadn't even considered an idea like this and was excited to meet and learn more about it. The rescheduled meeting seemed to be coming at the right time. The group finally looked as if it would be moving ahead.

⌇ ⑥ ⌇

'Savin' the Earth, one bag at a time' eh? Or was it 'Savin' the Earth, one bag of dog food at a time'? Both of 'em sound pretty catchy if ya' ask me. It's funny, but the guys'll end up holdin' onto that phrase durin' this whole process. They'll use it to remind themselves of their goal to create a truly all natural pet food. Besides, each time someone says it, they get a little chuckle. And sometimes a bit of levity sure don't hurt.

Now, if ya' haven't been able to tell, things're heatin' up. Ya' know the old sayin', "Two heads are better than one?" In this case, it rings clear as a bell. Mark had the spark of an idea but couldn't get it to start a full blown fire. Nick, on the other hand, couldn't strike a match to save his life, but when Mark gave him just a little spark, he managed to get things burnin'. And now, our guys're headin' down a path that'll soon take 'em somewhere completely off of their map. Ya' see, in their minds right now, all they're doing is writin' a grant, draftin' a proposal and hopin' the darned thing'll fly. None of 'em've thought much farther ahead than that. None of 'em can foresee where this'll take 'em. But I can, and ya'd better come along if ya' want to find out what happens.

Chapter 15 ⑥

At the last meeting, the guys decided it might be a good idea to head off to the bakery and check things out for themselves. After all, they didn't have a whole lot of time left. So, off they went and back they came. A fruitful visit found them returning with more information than they knew what to do with, some fresh baked goods, and smiles on their faces. The folks at the bakery had been extremely helpful and had also been baking breads for several years. Their operation ran smoothly. Their business plan utilized farm products purchased directly from farmers who were all members of the cooperative and had a vested interest in the success of the company. So, all Martin, Nick, and Mark had to do was change the bakery into a pet food factory and the bread into pet food. The plan was sound.

It took a couple of weeks after their visit to write everything up. Nick and Martin sent all of their information to Mark who put it together in an organized presentation package. He, after all, was the one with the most experience in that department. As soon as Mark had the presentation compiled, he overnighted Nick and Martin copies. When the delivery man dropped the package off on Martin's doorstep, he actually became a bit nervous. The strawberry guy, the food consultant guy, the man working towards a cause, actually got a bit nervous. A lot of time and energy had been spent on this plan. A lot of hope rested on its shoulders.

Martin didn't make it back inside the house before his curiosity got the best of him. Coffee in hand, he sat right down on his front doorstep and ripped open the envelope. As Martin scoured the materials, he was delighted at what he found. It was perfect. The plan, the presentation, the layout, everything was perfect. It had to be the best business proposal he had ever helped create, and now, after seeing what Mark had done with all the materials, he was even more impressed. The idea was sound. The pet food company would change the way these ranchers and farmers did business. They would make more money, reinvest in their operations and continue to grow. And that's not even the best part. The farmers would be able to continue to farm in a sustainable, earth-friendly manner, their cows would continue to be treated humanely, and their dogs would eat great food. Everything had fallen into place nicely, accomplishing the goals that the guys had set out to reach.

If one of Martin's neighbors had seen him on his doorstep that morning, they might have thought that he had won the lottery or inherited a grand sum of money from a long, lost uncle. Martin beamed. The smile on his face said it all. Now all he wanted was to call an emergency meeting of the rancher's group and give them the presentation immediately. They might as well get things started as soon as possible. He knew that this group of farmers would jump at the chance to involve themselves in such a sound plan. *At last,* he thought to himself. *At last this cause is picking up speed.*

ॐ ⑥ ॐ

Now, I don't have much to say at this point that hasn't already been said. But let me see if I can put a few things into perspective. First off, these guys've been workin' hard. And the funny thing is, none of 'em stand to make a single penny from compilin' all this research and draftin' this proposal. Once the ranchers co-op took hold of the pet food company, the guys'd be done. They'd be movin' on and findin' somethin' else to do. The interestin' thing about it, however, was that none of 'em really cared. When they started, they all knew that this was just one project and that at some point, the project'd come to an end. They knew they'd be getting' back to doin' whatever it was they were doin' before. But, for the time bein' they knew that this'd been the right thing for each of them to do. And now, as the presentation draws near, I think we should all sit back, take in a deep breath, and relax right along with our three everyday, ordinary people. It's been a job well done.

Chapter 16

At breakfast, the morning of the presentation, the group sipped their coffee and discussed the upcoming day.

"Mark, I know I've already told you this, but the format and presentation of all of this plan is just fantastic. You did an excellent job of pulling all of our random notes together," Martin said.

"Hey, if it weren't for you guys, I don't know what I'd be doing. I had a great time putting this stuff together. It's a great plan. Let's hope they go for it," Mark replied.

"You know guys, I think this plan is fantastic, but last night, when I was laying in bed, I got a a little worried," Nick said.

"Worried? About what?," Martin asked.

"Well, I've spent quite a bit of time with ranchers and farmers. I'm thinking that this idea might be a bit too big for them. Maybe a bit too big for them to get their arms around."

"But you, yourself said you thought this plan was sound," Mark said.

"It is sound. It's as sound as it can be. It's a great plan and I think it would work wonders for everyone involved. I just think we need to keep our optimism tabled for a bit. We want these ranchers to embrace this venture and get it going, but to do that, we've got a bit of a sales job to do. And yes, I have no doubt that the pet food company can be wildly successful and follow right in the same steps as Jerry's Bakery. But, I also know ranchers and often times they've got a bit of tunnel vision. They want to know that the weather's going to be favorable and that they're going to sell their cattle for the highest price."

"Ahh, the voice of reason, ladies and gentleman, Nick Patterson," joked Martin. "C'mon Nick, they'll go for it. How can they not?"

"Yeah, I know. I know. I don't want to bring anyone down. I just want to go into this realistically. On paper this pet food thing looks bulletproof. The farmers'll get a premium price for more of their meat. And, we have the bakery as a perfect example of success. But there's a possibility they won't like it," Nick added.

"How can they not like it? It's flawless. Shoot, I'd run this company if I could," Mark said.

"Let's hope they do," Martin said looking at his watch. "It's time. Let's pay our bill and head across the street. Gentleman, we're almost there. It's been a pleasure stumbling through the world of agriculture with you. Here's to the cause."

The grouped clinked their coffee mugs, took one last sip and headed for the door.

Slam dunk! Right? Well, maybe not just yet. Across the street right now the guys're meetin' with a group of ranchers whose main concerns're the weather and cattle prices. Unfortunately, Nick'd been right. The ranchers hadn't come to listen to three outsiders tell 'em to start producin' kibble. They didn't care about other folks and their darn bakery. They weren't about to start makin' pet food.

Are ya' stunned? I am. Each time I get to this part of the story I feel like someone hit me below the belt. It amazes me that some folks just can't see the gosh-darned forest for the gosh-darned trees. Some folks just can't grab a hold of somethin' different and let it carry 'em somewhere new. This time, it looks like we've got a bunch of ranchers who forgot to get in their four wheel drives when they headed out to the muddy fields. Now, they're stuck.

Ain't this swell? Ahh, well... What're ya' goin' to do? Ya' can't change people, now can ya'? Cattle farmers're cattle farmers, after all. Let's just hope our guys don't leave the meeting too discouraged. By the looks of how many pages're left in this story, they just might bounce back. (And yes, you saw that right. I did just wink.)

Chapter 17

Martin, Mark, and Nick slumped around a tall, circular table at a bar and restaurant across the street from the conference room they had been in most of the day. Abandoned suit coats hung from the backs of their chairs. Ties hung loosely and shirt tails dangled, untucked. The group looked like they hadn't slept in weeks. None of them seemed to mind that it was quiet and dark and empty in the bar.

Mark spoke first. "I feel like throwing our proposal off the bridge."

"How could they not accept it?" Martin asked.

"I just don't get it. Anyone in the corporate world would've jumped at our proposal. It's built to be successful," Mark stated.

"What a disappointment," Nick said. "And I hate to say this guys, and I sure hope I didn't jinx us this morning, but I really think the idea was just too big for them. I don't think they could see past their own pastures on this one," Nick said.

"But don't they realize that this plan helps them be successful? More successful?" Martin's voice rose. "Don't they realize we're trying to help them out? And that we believe in what they're doing?"

"Actually, I got the impression they were pretty impressed with the work. They even said we'd done an excellent job. But I also got the impression that they had no idea how to go about making pet food and that they weren't about to learn how. Most of them have been raising cattle for a long time. That's what they know. It's a different mentality. Pet food isn't something they know. It's just what they feed their pets," Nick said. "And maybe that's where we went wrong. We didn't put ourselves in their shoes enough and try to view this plan through their eyes. I don't know. Maybe we got blinded by our own plan."

"Well, it's a pretty darned frustrating mentality," Mark said. "Do they have any idea how much time we've spent on this? Can't they see Jerry's Bakery as a perfect example?"

"Bread's not dog food. Cattle producers don't grow wheat. It's still a different mentality," Nick said. "Maybe if we'd suggested creating a butcher shop, the idea would've flown better. Of course, it wouldn't've helped them much because they still would-n't have a place to sell their scrap meat."

"So what do we do now? Do we just let this whole thing drop?" Mark asked.

"What else are we going to do with it? I don't know any other ranchers who might be interested," Nick replied. "I guess we just shake hands, part ways, and hope something else pops up that we might be able to apply this to. I know I'll be looking for some-thing that it fits with, even if it isn't cattle. Maybe some other agricultural group would be interested. Some group in vegetables or fruits. I don't know."

"Hold on a second. Don't you think we've put too much work into this to let it just drop? I mean, this is a completely viable business venture. We can't just let it go and hope something else comes along. I'm tired of waiting," Martin said.

"I think Nick might be right. Maybe we can find some other farm groups and adjust the proposal to fit their needs," Mark said.

"Another farm group is about the last thing I want to deal with right now. I've already had the door closed in my face by two of them. I'm not going to give a third group the opportunity," Martin replied.

"Well, what other choices do we have? Do *you* want to make pet food?" Nick asked.

Martin's eyes twinkled a bit and a smile lit up his face.

"Oh no, I don't like the look on your face," Mark said.

"Hey Martin, I was just being sarcastic. I didn't really mean it," Nick said. "But I might," Martin replied. "Actually, the thought crossed my mind earlier today when it looked like we weren't getting anywhere with the ranchers."

"But we don't know anything about making dog food," Mark said.

"Of course we do. We've spent months researching it. The only thing we don't have is a processing facility," Martin said.

"Or any financial backing, or any pet food formulas, or…" Mark said.

"Okay, okay, I know. There's still work to be done, but think about it. Couldn't we take all of our information here and still achieve our initial goal? Don't we still want to help family farmers and ranchers so they can continue to provide us with healthy, natural food? Don't we want to encourage responsible farming that looks after the earth instead of abusing it?" Martin asked. "Don't we want to 'Save the Earth, one bag of dog food at a time'?"

"But I don't have any experience with these sorts of things," Nick replied.

"And I can't keep working for peanuts forever," Mark said.

"I still haven't heard a good reason from you guys as to why we can't start our own pet food company. We could turn around and buy the meat from the very group that just turned down our plan? We'd still be achieving our goal," Martin said. "Mark, if I remember correctly, you said before the meeting that you'd jump at a chance to run a company like this. What do you think?"

"I don't know Martin. I don't know if I have the energy to start up another company. Besides, we don't have much money to work with," Mark replied. "The grant money is all but gone. I've got a family and no real job. I can't afford to invest in a company right now. And, I need to start making some real money."

"Yeah, I really don't have money to be putting towards a company, either," Nick said.

"Okay, but what if I do?" Martin replied. "What if I help get the ball rolling by kicking in some money? I don't know how much I can actually put in, but I think I have a big enough chunk that would let us get organized enough to allow us to look for investors. It would probably be enough to carry us for about 6 months."

"I really need to be finding a job, though Martin," Mark said. "This was only supposed to be an interim thing."

"Why don't you let this be your job, Mark?" Martin asked. "We can use the startup money to pay your salary and you can organize everything. Nick and I can continue to feed you info and you can devote your time to bringing this company to life, something you know how to do really well. If the money runs out and we don't get anywhere, we'll cut our losses and leave it. But I believe, and I know you guys believe, that this plan has merit. We can make this a success. C'mon you guys. I've come too far with all of this to let it die. We've come too far. We can make some real progress here and truly help out these farmers. You both believe in this cause as much as I do. We're fighting the good fight."

"But we just told you that we can't invest right now, Martin," Nick said.

"It doesn't matter. Listen. This whole thing is much bigger than money. I know I'm taking a bit of a financial risk here, but I see it as a very calculated risk. We've done most of the planning already and everything seems to work. The money will work itself out one way or the other. Two things are possible. I lose my investment and we part ways knowing that we did our best. Or, I don't lose my investment and we create a company that makes a real impact in the meat industry and possibly has a ripple effect across the rest of the food industry. I've been trying to make headway in this organic, natural farming industry for quite a while. This is a way to do it. I'm sure of it," Martin said.

"But what if it fails?" Mark asked.

"All good entrepreneurs fail from time to time. If it fails, it fails. We move on, shake hands, pat each other on the back, learn from our mistakes and hopefully regroup at a later date for a new project. I think we work really well as a group. We each bring a different bit of expertise to the table and we all believe in the cause. It's too important to just drop. Don't you think?" Martin asked.

"You sure you don't want to go down the street and get a job selling cars?" Nick joked. "You're selling me on this idea and I haven't had a test drive yet."

"Listen. Why don't we get something to eat. During dinner, we'll talk about anything other than pet food and cows. We'll let this other stuff bounce around in our heads for a little while. After dinner, if we feel like bringing it back up, we can," Martin said. "If we need to take a couple of days to decide, we take a couple of days. Another day or two won't make a difference."

"I'm all for getting some food," Nick said. "I'm hungry. But I don't think I need to wait. We've said over and over again how good this plan is. We've put a lot of time and energy into it. I can't see why we wouldn't give it a shot. What've we got to lose?"

"That's what I like to hear. But seriously Nick. If you need to take a couple of days to think it over, do so." Martin replied. "And Mark, I'm not looking for an instant answer from you. If you need a little time, take it."

"I don't need anymore time, Martin," Nick replied. "And Mark, it'll be difficult to do this without you, but like Martin said, if you need some time, take it."

"I don't know guys. I'm feeling a bit left out." Mark replied knowingly. "Martin's all gung ho. Nick, you're jumping in. I'm not sure I have much choice," Mark paused and smiled at the guys. "Alright, I don't think I'll regret this. The plan is solid and as long as I can pull in a bit of a salary as we get into this, I should be able to hold on for awhile. You guys are both right. What do we have to lose?"

"I'll need a little money from time to time and money to cover travel expenses," Nick said with a smile. "But I should be able to make do with my other side projects. When do we want to have our 'first' meeting?"

"Aren't we having it right now?" Martin said with a grin. And at that, he reached into his coat pocket and pulled out his pen.

Grabbing a cocktail napkin off the table, he handed the napkin and the pen to Mark. "With your expertise in starting up the dairy company, it only seems fitting that you take the lead here. Don't you agree Nick?"

"Yep, seems fitting to me. I don't have much experience with this sort of thing. I'm just the farm guy, remember?" Nick replied.

"Yeah, we remember. You're the guy who jinxed us," Martin joked.

"Hey, I'm just a realist, that's all," Nick replied.

"And we love your Midwest sensibility, Nick. Now, Mark, why don't you write up an agreement and we'll all sign it," Martin said.

"On a napkin, Martin? Is this really the right way to start up a company?" Mark chuckled.

"Hey, it's better than toilet paper!" Martin retorted. "I left my briefcase in the car and I'm too tired to go get it. This'll work just fine. We'll back into this project, create a company that turns around and buys the trim, hearts, and livers from the farmers and show them what a difference it makes in their profitability. If we become a success, our pet food company will play a critical role in saving sustainable family farms, eliminating the use of antibiotics and hormones, and helping keep our land and water supplies clean. Ultimately we'll help to continue to make sure that there is healthy, fresh food available for more people. We'll take the bakery idea ten steps further. We'll not only create a successful pet food company, we'll be saving the planet right along with it. The cause will grow as a result of our work. And maybe, just maybe, other organic farmers will look at our business model and see it as a viable one. Fruit growers could make and bottle juices, vegetable growers could create their own packaging plants. The possibilities are endless."

"So, you really think this is a good idea, then?" Mark joked as he started jotting an agreement down on the napkin. "Do you think we'll be able to purchase a few legal pads with the start up money? I don't think I can rely on napkins for everything." Everyone laughed.

"I tell you what. I'll personally deliver a case to your doorstep as soon as we sign this napkin and have some dinner," Martin replied. "So we all agree. We'll put our time and effort into creating a new company. We'll probably need to look for at least one other person to help us get this off the ground. Think about that. Also, we'll need to come up with a name soon," Martin said. "Any suggestions?"

"Umm, how about 'Superhero Pet Foods'? And our slogan, "Saving the Earth, one bag of dog food at a time!" Nick replied as everyone laughed.

As the discussion continued, each member of the new company signed an agreement on a beverage napkin agreeing to devote their time and energy to seeing this company become a success. Mark would take over as the CEO. Nick and Martin would take on major support roles and start looking at the process of actually making pet food.

༅ ⑥ ༅

Well, well, well. What've we got here? Pretty flowers do actually grow out of cow manure sometimes. I'm thinkin' maybe ya' didn't see this comin'. Or, maybe ya' did. I guess it doesn't really matter, now, does it? Ya' see, even though our three heroes had no idea where the grant might lead 'em, they all knew that somethin' positive, maybe even somethin' really big, was in the works. With the rancher's co-op turnin' 'em down, the ol' ball might've slowed down a bit and bumped into a few obstacles, but ya' can be sure it kept on rollin'. And, our cause, (yes, our cause, because I know if yer still readin', ya've now embraced the cause) is pushin' that ball on down the road. But, before we all get too carried away, if this story has taught ya' anythin', it's not to get yer hopes up too high, just yet. There's a heck of a lot of work to be done. We might lose someone from the group, we're definitely goin' to attract a few more people to our cause, and things're goin' to get interestin'. I do hope ya' stay with us. *(Oh yeah, and before we move on. Before Martin flew out of town, he made a quick stop at Mark's house and left a fresh case of yellow legal pads on his front doorstep with a note attached.)*

PART TWO

Chapter 18 ⑥

The day after his flight home, Martin found himself a bit wound up. He spent the morning locked in his office writing ideas down, scratching ideas out, and writing down some more. After filling up a few pages of notes, he still felt like his wheels were spinning. When it came right down to it, starting up a pet food company seemed a bit overwhelming. *How did we go from grant writers to company owners over night?* Martin thought. *I'm not sure we're ready for this. Shoot, I'm not sure three guys are going to be able to pull all of this off before the money runs out. We're going to need more help especially when it comes to marketing and sales. But who? Who will we find that will believe in the cause and be able to give us the support that we need? We don't want to hire just anyone. The person has to understand what we are trying to do and support it fully. I guess my first step will be going through the rolodex. We found Mark that way. I'll get to that just as soon as I send an email to Nick and Mark.*

Nick and Mark,
Here's a list of things I came up with this morning. I think we need to take a look at them first. You've both probably gone through

several of these already, but I thought I'd take the time to jot them down and shoot them off. Let me know if you think I'm on track. We're still scheduled to meet next week in Colorado Springs. In the meantime, I'm going to go through my address book and see if there are any names that pop up for people who might be interested in joining the team. We need someone who has a strong advertising and marketing background and most importantly, someone who believes in our cause. Let me know if you think of anyone. If we're lucky, maybe we'll find someone before next week's meeting. Let me know if you need anything. And remember, we're 'Saving the Earth, one bag of dog food at a time'.

—MT

Things we need to do:
1. *Name the company and create a vision for the company. (Do this first.)*
2. *Create and name a dog food and take a look at cat food. (Where do we find dog food recipes? Will we use any protein sources other than beef?)*
4. *Get a natural meat source. (Nick, you have direct connections with all sorts of people in the meat industry.)*
5. *Find everything there is to know about the pet food market.*
6. *Create a marketing strategy in order to recruit investors (Check your list of contacts and make some calls.)*

p.s. Mark, do you have enough paper now?

After the email was sent, Martin settled down a bit more. At least he had a few things off his mind, if only temporarily.

Opening his rolodex, he started flipping through the A's, moved onto the B's and kept on going. Name after name of competent people popped up but none of them seemed to be the right match. Until, that is, Martin got to the P's. *Benjamin Pollard,* Martin thought. *Now there's a guy we just might be able to work with. I wonder how Ben's doing these days? He not only has a big heart, he's got some of the best marketing skills in the field.*

Martin thought about Ben for a minute. He didn't have anything to lose by calling him. Besides, he figured, if Ben couldn't help directly, he might know someone who could. Picking up the phone to call Ben, Martin took a deep breath and dialed the phone. *Everything will work,* he told himself. *Everything will work.*

Benjamin Pollard had been the managing director of a well-known advertising agency and had done work for many high-profile companies. One of his specialties was creating unique brands for new products. From the times Martin had met with Ben he remembered him as being someone with a lot of energy and drive. Ben also had a reputation as a straight shooter. He told it how it was and if you didn't like it, too bad. Don't get in his way. You're either with him or you get dropped off at the next bus stop. But underneath all that drive, there was a man who really cared about doing things the right way.

"Hello, this is Ben."

"Ben, it's good to hear your voice. This is Martin Trotter."

"Martin Trotter. It's sure good to hear from you. How are things out there in sunny southern California?"

"Sunny as usual. How's the Big Apple this time of year?"

"Temperamental. One day it's nice, the next it's overcast and feels like evil is floating above us in the clouds. Anyway, I hear you're working on some sort of new project. What's that all about?"

"Boy, word sure travels fast," Martin said. "It's a pet food company. It's still pretty new. I haven't told many people about it. How'd you hear?"

"Oh, just a guess, really. You seem to have a new project going each time I talk to you. Besides, there's actually a little buzz going around that you're working on something new."

"Well, since you seem to know more about my project than I do," Martin joked. "Why don't you come and join us? It's actually the reason I'm calling. We need someone like you to help us get this thing off the ground."

"Well, tell me a little bit more about it. I don't know a thing about dog food or cat food except for what I see in my dog's dish. I might be able to help in some way or another, though."

"Well, here's what we have so far..." Martin began to give Ben a brief timeline of events. He explained that this was a start-up company, that there wasn't a lot of money available right now, but that this whole idea about pet food helping family farmers was original. He also mentioned that the return on the investment had great possibilities.

"When do I start?" Ben asked.

"Excuse me?" Martin asked.

"When do I start?" Ben asked a bit more slowly and jokingly.

"Are you serious? You're really interested?"

"Yeah, it sounds like something I can sink my teeth into," Ben replied.

"Well, I can overnight all of our information and research to you. Do you think you can make our meeting next week? Maybe you and I can fly in a day early and go over everything before you meet Nick and Mark. We usually meet at this great little diner for breakfast and work from there. The waitresses take good care of us. So far we've been able to meet once a month or so and do everything else through email and phones. It seems to work. I'm sure we'll need to start meeting more, but until then, we'll stick with this plan.

"This sounds like an amazing project. I'm used to doing things on a "for profit" basis only. I haven't been involved in a project that looks like it can turn a profit and also help people at the same time. And, if it gets healthier food to dinner tables, it sounds great. It would be wonderful if organic foods were available at the prices that other foods are."

"That's one of the main reasons we're all doing this. And as we've been working on it, we keep seeing other areas that we'll be able to impact. We'll have healthier food for dogs and cats. Cattle will be treated more humanely, more natural meat will be available because the farmers will be able to expand production, and who knows what might also come up," Martin replied. "I'll overnight you the information along with a ticket to Colorado. Call me or email me if you have any questions at all."

"Excellent. I'll see what I can come up with. Thanks for thinking of me. It'll be good to do something that has some real heart to it."

As Martin hung up the phone he leaned back in his chair and smiled. *One more for the cause!* He couldn't wait to hear from Ben about what he thought. He couldn't wait for Ben to meet the rest of the group. Another piece had fallen in place.

⌁ ⑥ ⌁

Now there's no doubt in my mind that our original three everyday ordinary people could've gotten this project off the ground on their own. It might've taken'em a bit longer on their own, but they're all capable, experienced people. And, capable experienced people also know that askin' for help's a sign of intelligence. Our guys ultimately knew that it'd be a much better choice to bring in some help, some fresh ideas. So, now we've come to that part in the story where Ben shows up. Ben'll stick around awhile too, designer suits and all. I really wish ya' could see 'em when they get together – jeans and hikin' boots, flip-flops and flowered shirts, cowboy hat and cowboy boots, and Gucci or Versace or both – they really are a sight.

Ben's goin' to add some needed fuel to the fire and help build a pet food brand that just might turn out to be pretty darn successful. As we move along now and get to know Ben, we'll also meet a few more everday ordinary people. But, I'd better not be gettin' too far ahead of myself. Shoot, ya' haven't even gotten to know Ben yet.

Chapter 19 ⑥

T he next meeting rolled in a couple of weeks after the napkin was signed and before anyone had a chance to take a breath. Ben had received his 'care package' complete with airline ticket. After the introductions over breakfast and some fine pancakes and sausage, the real meeting got underway. Martin, Nick, Mark, and now Ben were ready for two days of non-stop brainstorming. Their main goal had been determined in several emails sent over the course of the week. The company had to be defined. And so, for the next couple of days, the guys would work to define the company's core ideals.

The group chose to make Denver their permanent meeting place. It was a good location for everyone. Nick and Mark were both from the greater Denver area which made it easy for Martin to fly in from Southern California. Ben was from New York which made Colorado a good halfway point between So. Cal and the Big Apple.

"So where are we at with things so far?" Mark asked as the guys seated themselves around a small round conference table in Martin's suite.

"Overwhelmed, that's where I am at," Martin replied. "This is going to be one heck of a project to pull off."

"Do you think we've bitten off more than we can chew?" Nick asked

Martin, forever the optimist in the group, replied, "Not at all. I think the idea is great. I think the plan is sound. It's just going to be a lot of work. I think we might be in over our heads a bit, but I'm certain we can pull it off. We're all experienced in one sense or another. Besides, we'll find others who'll help us round out our lack of information and experience. We've already dragged Ben into it. We'll figure it out. The pet food industry's been around for years and we have enough business experience and knowledge of the farming industry to pull this off well. I keep thinking about how many people we might possibly help and that's what keeps me coming back to the belief that we can do this."

"Yeah, I guess I'm right there with you Martin," Nick said. "I've spent the past week thinking all of this over and asking myself how I got into this mess, but I keep coming back to the farmers. Imagine if we create a business model for natural food that gets used by other people in the organics business? And in doing that, more natural food gets produced and gets into the hands of the general customer. We could, and I know it might take a while, impact the way people eat in this country. We could impact the way farming happens in this country. Wouldn't it be great if we could get away from factory farms altogether? Or at least force them to change their practices? We have the potential to affect change in our communities."

"When I returned home and told my wife what we were doing and why we were doing it, she hesitated at first. She'd like me to find a job that has some stability. We talked it over quite a bit and the more I talked it through, the more it made sense. And, the more important it seemed. I feel we really have to give this a shot. I also think that our plan has potential." Mark said. "And, quite honestly, I'm thrilled to be a part of it. What if we become successful and help to change the way the farming industry approaches things? What if most of the vegetables at the grocer were organic and you had to go to the little 'pesticide section' to get your vegetables and fruit sprayed with some refreshing herbicides and pesticides?" Everyone laughed.

"I'm just excited to be included in all of this," Ben added. "I haven't been able to stop thinking about this stuff since Martin called me last week. I've looked over everything and it looks great. I think you guys have something completely doable. And I know Mark was joking a bit there, but imagine, just imagine the possibilities. We could make an impact."

Everyone seemed to relax a bit after they had each spoken. Everyone was in it for the right reasons. Everyone was in it for the cause. As a result, as they got down to work, the energy in the room flowed. For two days straight, they worked, coming up for air to call their families and get a bite to eat. By dinner on the second night, they had their company defined. 'Pure Pet' was born.

Pure Pet Standards and Principles

Mission

To change the way animals are raised (no hormones, antibiotics or factory farming) and to change the way our pets are fed (no rendered animal by-products).

Pure Pet will enhance the health and well-being of animals with the most nutritionally pure pet foods available. Our products will offer complete nutrition. We support sustainable ranching practices and family farmers. We will promote the development of naturally raised livestock without the use of added hormones, antibiotics, artificial additives, or animal based feeds.

Brand Construction

Our brand will be constructed from the inside out. How we relate to others, our animals and the planet will become the voice of our company, a voice the consumer listens to.

The company/brand is the collective vibration of its employees. Individually, what will each person do to inspire others towards Pure Pet's mission, principles, and values?

Pledges We Make...and Keep

We strive to improve the quality of life for all companion animals.

We insist on the humane treatment of all animals.

We live out our mission in our personal and professional lives.

We support family farmers and ranchers who are dedicated to raising livestock without the use of added growth hormones, antibiotics, and animal-sourced feeds.

We work with family ranchers and farmers to expand practices that ensure humane care of all livestock.

We sponsor organizations working for the sustainable use of our natural resources, and for the humane care of all animals.

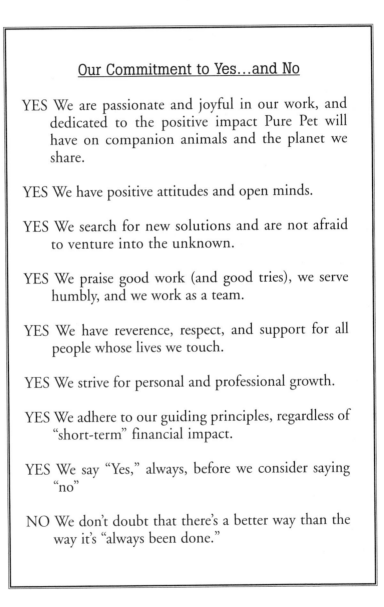

Our Commitment to Yes...and No

YES We are passionate and joyful in our work, and dedicated to the positive impact Pure Pet will have on companion animals and the planet we share.

YES We have positive attitudes and open minds.

YES We search for new solutions and are not afraid to venture into the unknown.

YES We praise good work (and good tries), we serve humbly, and we work as a team.

YES We have reverence, respect, and support for all people whose lives we touch.

YES We strive for personal and professional growth.

YES We adhere to our guiding principles, regardless of "short-term" financial impact.

YES We say "Yes," always, before we consider saying "no"

NO We don't doubt that there's a better way than the way it's "always been done."

ༀ ⑥ ༀ

Not bad for a bunch of guys who didn't know each other a while back. These guys're driven by a purpose bigger than all of 'em combined. Heck, they're driven by a purpose bigger than all of us. Boy, this story sure grabs yer attention, don't it? Take a look back for a minute. Ya' got guys sprayin' strawberries with all sorts of chemicals and sellin' 'em to the general public. Ya've got factory farms feedin' cows a cheap diet and then injectin' 'em with growth hormones and antibiotics just so they can get 'em to the slaughterhouse more quickly. Ya've got good guys who get the door slammed in their faces, not once, but twice, who then, even when the chips're down, turn around and make somethin' good. Don't ya' just love a story like that? I bet the natural meat farmers're goin' to be glad to hear from these guys as soon as they start makin' pet food.

For now, however, our guys've got a lot of work ahead of 'em. They've got to take the seed of their company and find someone who has some money so they can make it grow. And yes, they've got a whole lot of other things to do, too, but I'm not goin' to bore ya' with all the nitty gritty details and conversations. Let's just say that there's no more time for messin' around. Our guys've got to pull the company together, write up a marketin' plan, and get themselves ready to start makin' pet food. So, seein' how we've just skipped all the borin' details, we might as well jump on ahead. Another hurdle's goin' to get in the way and the guys're goin' to have to figure out how to get over it.

Chapter 20

Martin's start up money had all but dried up. The guys all knew that the success of the company hinged on finding an investor, but with most of the money gone, and nobody beating down their door, things didn't look too promising. As they met at the diner for their next monthly meeting, a meeting that could potentially be one of their last, none of them glowed with the energy they had shared just a few months back when they had formed 'Pure Pet.' To top things off, the day wasn't going to start off much better. As they ordered their breakfasts, checked up on each other's families, and shared news, Mark broke in.

"Hey guys, I don't mean to interrupt, but I have some good news and I have some bad news. Which do you want first?" Mark asked.

"Good news first. Always good news first," Martin replied.

"Well, I've just signed on with a different company as their CEO. I didn't want to say anything until I knew for sure. But it's a company that can actually pay me to work. Martin, you've been great getting all of this started and taking care of us in terms of the time we've put in. But, even with your generosity, my wife and I have still been struggling. I needed to find a job that had a bit more security, some benefits, and the ability to pay me a higher salary. I understand that this comes at a time when things are just ramping up, but I don't see us finding an investor for another couple of months and if I wait around for the unknown, well…you understand, right?"

"You're leaving?" Nick said. "You've been in this thing for quite some time. You've got a lot of time invested in this. Are you sure this is what you want to do?"

"I'm pretty torn, actually," Mark replied. "This hasn't been an easy decision, but when I start thinking about the possible financial damage that my family could experience because of all of the unknowns, I really don't have much choice. Besides, the company I'm going to work for has a strong sense of social responsibility. I think it'll be a good fit for me. I won't be fighting exactly the same fight, but it'll be close."

"But who's going to do everything that you've been doing?" Martin asked. "None of us can handle the types of things that you've been handling like you do."

"Well, I'm not going to just run out the door as soon as I'm finished telling you this. I'll help with the transition. Besides, you'll make it work. Remember, this project is bigger than all of us."

"Ahh, my own words coming back to bite me," replied Martin.

"Mark, we all have families. We understand. We hate to see you go, but we understand," Nick said.

"I waited as long as I could because I really believe in Pure Pet. I don't doubt that you guys will make it successful, but I…"

"Mark, we'll manage. We know we're in cash-flow limbo right

now. We understand. We're disappointed, but you have to take care of you and your family first. There were no guarantees with this from the beginning," Martin said.

"I hate to do this. I'll be here for the next couple of days to get everybody up to speed as to what I've been doing. After that, you know that if there are any problems, you can call me and I'll gladly help if at all possible. Pure Pet has a remarkable plan in place. I think we've done an excellent job of getting everything in order. You guys'll just have to man this boat without me. I do expect to be kept in the loop, however. I do believe in this cause and I'll be the first one in line to purchase the food as soon as it hits the market. And hey, maybe someday when you're all basking in the success of Pure Pet, you'll be able to pay me more and hire me back," Mark said.

꒜ ⑥ ꒜

I really hated to do that to ya'. But a storyteller's got to tell the story the way it happened. Our boys spent the next couple of days feelin' a bit down in the mouth. Nobody wanted Mark to leave. If ya' remember, he's the one who found *them*. He's the one who got everythin' organized and started with the grant. The guys saw him not only as a colleague, but also as a friend. And as friends, they understood that Mark had to do what was best for him and his family. After all, takin' care of the family's why most of us get outta' bed and trudge off to work each day. Anyway, nobody was excited about Mark leavin'.

By the end of the last couple of days with Mark, all the loose ends got tied up. The business plan and the marketin' materials were ready to go. Martin reluctantly took over where Mark left off becomin' Pure Pet's new CEO. Nick and Ben thought he was the best man for the job.

After our boys said goodbye to Mark, they agreed upon one thing. They needed to find someone to invest in Pure Pet. So, for the next few weeks, that's what they set about doin' – makin' phone call after phone call after phone call.

Chapter 21

The guys missed Mark quite a bit. He'd taken care of a lot of the logistical work for the team. After Martin had taken over many of the duties, he delegated the rest to Nick and Ben. Overall, things looked good. It was, however, difficult to lose a main support person. With his extra responsibilities, Martin felt busier than he had in months. He'd spent more time in his office in the several weeks since Mark left than he could ever remember. As he sat going through paperwork one day, the phone rang. It was Ben.

"Martin. I've got great news. We've been putting the word out and making calls and coming up empty, but I think I might've struck gold. I've arranged a dinner meeting with Phil Lankford. He's interested in Pure Pet and may be able to get us the money that we need."

"That's great Ben, when do we meet? Wait a second. Did you say Phil Lankford?"

"Yep, Phil Lankford's interested in what we've got going. Can you believe it? I scheduled the meeting for the Wednesday night of our next meeting. Beforehand, we'll have a chance to meet and strategize before we go meet him. I'm pretty excited about this. I think we have a shot at taking Pure Pet a step further."

"Have you spoken to Nick yet?"

"I haven't gotten a chance to call him."

"Well, I have some other things to discuss with him. I'll tell him when I call later if you don't mind."

"Perfect. Finally, things are looking up. It's too bad Mark couldn't hold out for a little while longer. I sure thought we were done for when he left. Anyway, our plan will grab Phil's attention. I'm certain of it. He sounded quite positive on the phone."

"Great. I can't wait. Keep me posted. I'll talk to you soon."

Martin hung up the phone. He wanted to jump out of his socks, but contained himself for the time being. He couldn't get too excited yet. But Phil Lankford? Phil Lankford was a mover and a shaker in the business world. He was a big man, both in stature and business prowess and seemed to always have his hand on the pulse of business. This could really turn into something big."

The next couple of weeks went by quickly. The group gathered on Tuesday and Wednesday to make sure everything was in order. By late Wednesday afternoon they were ready. Their hopes were high and they believed in their cause. Ben, with all of his experience in marketing would take the lead. Martin and Nick would fill in where they were needed. They left the hotel to meet Phil. When they entered the restaurant, the maitre d' ushered them into the lounge where Phil waited for them. Ben approached Phil first.

"Phil, it's good to see you. We have to thank you for meeting with us. We're all pretty excited to finally share Pure Pet with someone else," Ben began.

Phil's voice resonated across the bar as he responded. "Benjamin Pollard. You had me so interested in this plan when we spoke on the phone, I forgot to ask. What's a guy like you doing outside of the world of advertising? And who're these gentlemen in tow behind you?"

"Phil, I'd like you to meet Martin Trotter and Nick Patterson. They're really the masterminds behind this whole thing. They brought me in as a hired gun!" Ben replied.

"It's a pleasure to meet you both," Phil said extending his hand to both of them. "I understand that you have spent most of your life in the food business, Martin. What brings you to pet food instead of people food?"

"Well, as we'll explain, the two industries are really quite inter-twined," Martin replied. "I've followed many of your ventures in the business sections for several years. It's a pleasure to finally meet you."

"And Nick, what's this I hear about you and a bunch of trac-tors taking over Washington, D.C. a few years back? I bet you've got some stories to tell," Phil said.

"I was a lot younger then. And yes, I might have a story or two to tell from those days if I can remember back that far," Nick answered. "I've heard a lot about you from Martin and Ben. It's good to meet you."

"Would anyone care for something to drink? I've arranged for us to meet in a private room so that we can have as much time as we need. I'm sure you three have plenty to keep me busy with for the next couple of hours. Not that the food, which is exquisite here, won't do that, but we are here for business after all."

The four men were ushered to the private room where Ben took the lead and introduced Pure Pet, its mission and the cause. Nick and Martin picked up where Ben left off and the meeting rolled smoothly along with Phil stopping occasionally to rave about the food and ask a question or two.

"You know," Phil began. "Just last week I had to sell our farm. It had been part of the family since the turn of the century. It's just about impossible to make any money in that business right now. It's unfortunate. We held onto it as long as we could, but it really had become a liability. I don't have time to farm it, nor do I really care to get my hands dirty anymore, and the folks we had living there and farming the property for us were too limited in the resources that they had. We would've had to invest large sums of money and hire more people if we were going to be at all competitive and turn a profit. We really just had to sell. Fortunately, one of the other small farmers up the road had been looking for more land in order to expand. At least I didn't have to sell to some factory farm operation."

"Then you know first hand where we're coming from," Martin stated.

"Oh, I definitely know. It broke my heart to sell off that land. My great grandfather farmed that land. My grandfather farmed that land. My father farmed that land. I was supposed to farm that land, but I took another career path. It was a major family issue when it came time to sell it," Phil said.

"Unfortunately, that's happening all over the country. Small farmers just can't compete," Nick said. "That's why we all got into this. This cause is much bigger than pet food. It encompasses responsible farming practices, a need for people to have healthy food, animal treatment, environmental issues, and a strong desire to make things right once again. If we can lead the way with our company, other companies might follow our lead. Hopefully we can put enough pressure on factory farms to change their practices. We've got lofty goals, but we believe that it's possible."

"Well, I believe it's possible too," Phil replied. "I'd like to see this company make it into production. I can arrange for about $500,000 so that you can have the ability to do the things you need to do in order to establish this as a real company. Also, you all mentioned Dr. Ball in your discussion when you talked about your research. I can arrange for you to meet her. It might be a great thing to have her on your dog food bag endorsing your product. Also, I know some folks at Howell University. They have a huge veterinarian research facility there and turn out some of the best vets in the country. I can arrange for you to meet with the director of research there and talk to him about your venture. The more I think about this, the more excited I'm getting about it. This has some real potential. We've got to think big about this one. If you want to make major change, which I believe you all want, you've got to think big. You've got to look at all the factors outside of the pet food world. Obviously, you've done that to a certain extent because your company exists because of problems in the farming industry, but you've also got to look at..."

"Can we back up a couple of steps here, Phil?" Martin interrupted. "Did you just tell us that you're going to arrange for us to receive about $500,000 dollars so we can continue?"

"Yep. That's what I said," Phil replied.

"I don't know how we can thank you," Martin replied as a broad smile lit up his face. "This is big. This is real big. We can actually make this company work. We keep finding people who believe in what we're doing and the door keeps opening. We've got some more work to do."

"Here's how you can thank me. Turn this company into something substantial. Help those farmers and produce a food that I can feed my Irish Setter. I don't want him eating rendered protein from god-knows-what kinds of sources."

"I think this calls for a bottle of champagne," Ben replied. "I can't wait to get going on this."

As the waiter brought a bottle of champagne, the guys gave a toast to Pure Pet, thanked Phil several times, and headed back to their hotel. They had just gotten the best news they could've imagined. Finally, after all the setbacks, it finally looked like they were getting somewhere.

Don't ya' wish that Mark'd been around for all of this? He would've really enjoyed it. He truly would've. And don't think the guys forgot about him and didn't call to let him know their progress. He was just about as excited as they were, and, I might add, he had a right to be. The company wouldn't have been able to get off the ground without him. Anyway, I'd better keep movin' on.

So, how about them apples, eh? Don't ya' just love it? Don't ya' just love it when people believe in somethin' strongly enough that good things happen and then other good people come along and want to help out? I sure do. And as things start to grow lots of other people get interested and then get involved. Phil's investment and his business contacts would allow the guys to move their company out of the plannin' stages and into the 'Hey-we-just-might-make-somethin'-out-of-this' stage. Good ol' Pure Pet's about to become a reality.

The next few months'll move pretty darn quick. Almost overnight they'll go from a company hangin' on by the skin of its teeth to a company that can only see the sunshine. A whole bunch of things'll start to happen. The guys'll contact Dr. Ball, who'll agree to endorse their product. In fact, her smilin' face, and a little blurb about why she likes Pure Pet, will turn up on every bag of pet food. Howell University'll agree to help with the different types of pet food recipes. Overall, things're fallin' into place. It's sure a whole lot nicer than things fallin' apart.

Chapter 22

Things moved right along until Martin received a call one sunny afternoon.

"Martin, we have a problem," Nick was on the other end of the line.

"What kind of problem are we looking at Nick?" Martin responded.

"Well, I've got a bunch contacts for natural meat suppliers but I can't find a single processing plant in this country that can verify that the meat they receive from the natural farmers will be the same meat that we receive to turn into dog food. They have no systems in place to accept meat and keep it separated. Whatever meat comes in goes into the same process and comes out the other end. Our natural meat will get mixed up with factory farm meat. We won't be able to make the claims we need to make about our pet food if we can't get this stuff certified. We have to be able to claim that there are no antibiotics, no hormones, no brain tissue, no spinal cord tissue, and no rendered by-products."

"This isn't the kind of news I was hoping to hear from you today, Nick. This sure messes things up. Our product is worthless without that source verification. I mean, what's the point in doing any of this if we can't guarantee that we use natural meat? Our whole cause gets lost which is the reason why we created this business in the first place," Martin replied. "Well, what do we do now? Do you know of anyone who might be able to help us?"

"I've been racking my brain and can't come up with anything or anyone. I can't tell you how many processing plants I've flown into or called. They all act like I'm crazy. I really am at a loss."

"Alright. I'll call Ben and run this by him. Call anyone you think might be able to help us. I'll do the same."

Pure Pet would have to call it quits if a processing plant couldn't be found to keep their meat separated. There was little chance that they could find an investor with really deep pockets who would enable them to start their own processing plant. Besides, building a processing plant would take too long. Once again, Pure Pet had its back against the wall.

Martin hadn't foreseen any problems like this. In fact, neither had Nick or Ben. After the meeting with Phil, things had moved along at a rapid pace. There had been few problems. Everything seemed like it was meant to be. But now what? *I guess I can do what I always do.* Martin thought to himself as he reached for his rolodex. *It's a good thing I've kept this thing updated over the years. Let's see who might pop his or her head out at me and smile. There's got to be someone in here who can help us out.* One thing Martin had learned early in his career was that it was a good idea to keep track of all of your business contacts. And this time, he was prepared to call everyone on the list. Pure Pet wasn't going to close up shop until they had exhausted all of their possible resources.

Later that day, Martin called Theresa Sturm, an up and coming business executive who Martin had worked with at

Companion Pet International (CPI), one of the world's largest pet food companies. Martin decided to give her a call. After he spent a few minutes catching up on old times, the discussion moved to Pure Pet. Martin explained everything about Pure Pet – the company's mission, their guiding principles, a little bit of company history – and then jumped into the main problem at the time.

"...so now that you know all of that information, Theresa, I called because we have a problem and I hoped maybe you'd be able to help," Martin said.

"Well, so far everything you've told me has been completely fascinating," Theresa sounded interested. "I love the cause. I'd also love to see Americans getting back to healthier diets and healthier living. This is a great way for small farms to make a stand."

"That's what we're hoping everyone who comes across our path thinks," replied Martin. "If people believe in this cause, those of us who are part of this company along with the consumer, can make some serious progress in getting farming back where it needs to be. Hopefully we can influence other parts of the farming industry to change also. And, maybe we'll even make an impact on the factory farms."

"So what is it that you need from me?" Theresa asked.

"Well Theresa, we have a major stumbling block. We can't find a processing plant anywhere that can guarantee that the natural meat we bring them will be the natural meat we get back. Our main claim is that our meats come from sources that don't use antibiotics and growth hormones, and that our protein sources have no brain and spinal tissue in them. Without being able to keep our protein sources clean, we're out of business.

Right now, and anytime in the near future, we don't have the capital to start our own plant, and it would take much too long to build one. We are at a loss as to where to go next."

"Well Martin, you may have called the right person, but I won't know until I make a couple of phone calls myself. Why don't I call you back later, either today or tomorrow and let you know what I come up with. I have a couple of ideas, but I'll have to check first. I don't want you getting your hopes up."

"Hey, I'll take a maybe," Martin replied. "It's better than 'no.' Thanks for helping out. I look forward to hearing from you soon."

"My pleasure, Martin. It's for a good cause. I'll talk to you soon."

As Martin hung up the phone, all he could do was hope and keep going through his rolodex. When he hadn't heard back from Theresa by early evening, he resigned himself to spending tomorrow on the phone again. He hoped that Nick and Ben were making some progress elsewhere.

After a restless night, Martin headed downstairs before his wife got up, made some coffee and headed into his quiet home office. His plan was to make a bunch of calls to people back east just when they'd be getting into their offices. Maybe he'd catch someone who was fresh and willing to listen. As he turned on his office lamp, sipped his coffee, and sat down in his chair, he noticed the message light blinking on his answering machine.

"Hi Martin, it's Theresa. I know it's late but I thought you might like to hear some good news. One of my contacts is very interested in your company. They want to talk with you as soon as possible. Please call me as soon as you get this, it doesn't matter what time."

Martin couldn't believe it. Theresa must have called back after he had headed upstairs for the evening. Picking up the phone, he dialed Theresa's number.

"Hello, this is Theresa."

"Theresa, it's Martin. Sorry I missed your call. I know it's early, but what's going on?"

"Hi Martin. I had hoped you'd pick up last night. I know I called a bit late, but I thought you might like the good news. I spoke with the President of Companion Pet International late yesterday afternoon. It turns out that they have a processing facility that would meet your needs. They make a line of specific diet foods that veterinarians sell and have a separate processing system for it. He's very interested in talking to you about Pure Pet. I explained everything to him about your company. It turns out that he grew up in a farming community in Nebraska. I hope I didn't overstep my boundaries, but he seemed so interested at the moment that I jumped at the chance and arranged a meeting for you next week on Thursday. Can you make it?"

"Can I make it? Of course I can make it. And no, you didn't overstep anything. Thank you. We'll be there. And they have a processing facility that will work for us? Nick'll jump for joy when he hears this. I can't thank you enough, Theresa."

"I'm just glad I can help out, Martin. You guys are working on something pretty special. I hope the meeting with CPI turns into something beneficial."

"It has to. I'm so glad I called you. When things settle down a bit, I'm buying you dinner."

"It would be good to see you again, Martin. Take care and call if you need anything else."

How d'ya' like that? Theresa and Martin hadn't spoken to each other in years and here she was, ready to help out. And guess what? She did more'n help out. Because of Theresa, Pure Pet'll live to see another day. In fact, it'll live to see many days. To make another long-winded business deal short, the folks at CPI liked the idea so much they made our Pure Pet boys an offer they couldn't refuse. In the blink of an eye, Pure Pet became a part of CPI, a big corporation with a lot of resources.

Can you believe it? Our guys found a corporation to help'em with their cause. A big corporation with operations in other countries. Almost seems a bit odd, don't it? I sure thought so when I first heard about it. I mean, why would our guys work with a big ol' company that probably still buys rendered proteins for its other lines of pet foods? Sounds a bit hypocritical, doesn't it? Aren't our guys workin' to get better food out to the public? Aren't our guys tryin' to help out small family farmers? What's goin' on here? I'm not so sure I can get my head wrapped around all of this.

Ya' know, when I first heard about this deal, I got myself a bit wound up. Wait a minute, now, I had to tell myself. Hold your horses. Maybe this isn't such a bad idea. Let's take a look at this. If this big corporation sells a lot of dog and cat food in every corner of our country, that means Pure Pet could very well walk into a pretty large market that already exists. A pretty large market would allow them to sell a lot of pet food. And, if they sell a lot of pet food they have to buy a lot of natural meat. And...well, do you see where I'm goin' with this? I guess at first, it almost seems like our guys are sellin' out. But they're really not. They're actually gettin' more help than they could've dreamed of. And, they're gettin' a big ol' corporation to help 'em out which means it's doin' somethin' good too. And maybe if this big corporations starts doin' somethin' good, others'll follow. I guess we'll just have to wait and see. Overall, this whole business deal might turn out to be a pretty darn good thing.

Besides, remember our guys? They're pretty smart. When they signed on with CPI, Pure Pet agreed to do things the way they'd been doin' 'em. In fact, that's the way the company president wanted it. He liked the guys so much that he'd only agree to help 'em if they stuck around and ran the company. He felt strongly that the guys had to continue their cause, besides, secretly he believed it was the only way this company was goin' to make it. And, he wanted it to make it. He wanted to be part of somethin' good. So that's why he wanted our guys to oversee everythin' and run things on their own. Ultimately, it'd be up to them whether Pure Pet made it or not. Besides, Martin, Nick, and Ben would'nt've had it any other way.

So, there ya' have it. We've come to the end. Four average everyday gentleman have put together a company, have had a few setbacks, and have finally sold it to an international corporation. What else is there to tell?

PART THREE

Interlude

Quite a bit actually. Ya' see, there's always been much more goin' on in our little tale than just sellin' pet food. Sure, it might be dressed up in a bag full of kibble, but what's inside that bag ain't crunchy little brown bits of food. No, inside that bag're people. Everyday ordinary folks, just like you and me. And ya' know, that's what this story's really been about the whole time I've been tellin' it. Behind the strawberries, behind the pesticides and the herbicides, behind the organic farmers and the factory farmers, there've always been folks who want to do somethin' good. Somethin' good like get more healthy, organic food into the market so your family and my family have healthier options each night when we sit down to dinner. Somethin' good like usin' fewer and fewer chemicals that seep into the groundwater supply and wash into our water sources after a big rain. Somethin' good like lookin' out for farm animals who can't really look out for themselves. And, along the way, those folks've wanted to bring along other folks, just like you and me, who want to do good also. And hopefully, just maybe, the good that's bein' spread around will grow and grow and grow. Wouldn't that be somethin'…

So, end of story? Naw. Where'd be the fun in that? I'm havin' too much fun to stop now. Besides, there's some interestin' stuff to happen, a few more lessons to learn, and some more everyday, ordinary people to meet.

Howard

As far as our story goes, Howard Sands comes along just about as soon as the ink dries on the contract that our boys signed with CPI. Howard's spent most of his life climbin' the corporate ladder and to tell ya' the truth, it's taken a bit of a toll on him. His hair's gotten a bit gray and it's not quite as thick as it used to be. His belly's gotten a bit soft and quite a bit bigger. Funny thing is, Howard used to take great pride in bein' fit and healthy. At one time he'd been an avid long distance runner competing in marathons around the country. Not anymore. About the only place he runs into each morning is the convenient store for a donut and coffee. I guess somewhere along the way he decided that work was just too darn important and he didn't have time for all of that other silly nonsense.

Now Howard's new job's to help Martin, Nick, and Ben get things goin'. He's supposed to be their link to CPI and show 'em the ropes. When he first got the phone call from his boss about it, he was tickled pink. Ya' see, he thinks this assignment'll put him one step from the top of the corporate ladder, and boy would he like to make it there. Shoot, since he started workin' at CPI, Howard's been eyein' the corner office on the top floor. Ya' know, the one with the view? And, he's played by all the rules to get there. He bought himself expensive suits and a fancy car and never missed an outside work function. In fact, he's made himself available to his job more often than he's made himself available to his family. One thing's for darn sure, Howard's a company man.

Jennifer

Jennifer Billings comes our way kinda' by accident. She hasn't worked in a corporate office for years. That's not to say she hasn't got any experience with it, though. At one time, she'd been on her way to becomin' a top executive. By the time her 30th birthday rolled around, she'd managed the publicity division of a well-established corporate event plannin' company. She flew all over the country meetin' with company bigwigs and worked long but rewardin' hours. And then one fine day, her husband started buggin' her about havin' kids. She did her best to hold him off for awhile, but somewhere along the way she found herself huggin' a beautiful little girl. And once that happened, things changed. Her life as a workin' professional took a back seat and left Jennifer wonderin' why she'd waited so long. She sure loved bein' a mom. And to tell ya' the truth, her kids turned out to be much more fun than company bigwigs.

Now, 12 years later, this pretty brown-haired mother of three's decided she might like to go back to work. The kids're all in school and the days at home're feelin' a bit empty. A part-time job just might give her somethin' to do, besides she might enjoy workin' with some adults for a change.

Somewhere along the way, not too long before our boys show up, Jennifer found her way to CPI. The folks in human resources were tickled pink that someone with her experience was lookin' to help out. They couldn't offer her much at first, but that was alright with Jennifer. She'd work wherever she was needed for the time bein'. The office was close to home and the nice folks at CPI'd agreed to let her work around her kids' schedule. Of course, it didn't take long for everyone around the office to take a likin' to her. She always wore a big smile and she always worked hard.

It still surprised her a bit, though, when Howard showed up one day askin' for help on a new project. She told him she'd think about it but it didn't take long for her to come to like the idea. She was ready for somethin' a bit more challengin' and this project sounded like a good one. She was hopin' to put some of her old skills to use with Pure Pet. The only thing she wasn't too sure about, though, was Howard. She'd met him a couple a' times before, but hadn't gotten a chance to work with him. He was kinda' known around the office as bein' a bit demandin'. She figured he couldn't be much worse than some of the company presidents she'd dealt with in the past and thought she'd be able to work around him. After all, the project sounded more interestin' all the time.

Elizabeth

When Martin'd talked to Elizabeth Campos about comin' to work with Pure Pet she hadn't been all that interested. Workin' as a representative for a pet food company didn't really sound too interestin'. Actually, she thought, it sounded a bit stiflin'. Besides, there'd be a lot of travelin' and she didn't like to fly. Her daddy'd gotten on an airplane every Monday mornin' and come home every Thursday night when she was growin' up. Over the years, she'd seen him get lost in his job and she sure didn't want that to happen to her. She was still young.

Besides, when it came down to it, Liz'd made other plans. Back in high school, this free spirited girl'd fallin' in love with her daddy's old camera. She'd be out snappin' pictures for hours, wanderin' the neighborhoods and parks, usin' up roll after roll of film. By the time she left home, she'd become a darn good photographer. From time to time, she'd even made a little money shootin' pictures for the local paper. She also got herself a scholarship to a fancy art school on the east coast, but within a year or so of graduatin', she'd realized that the business side of takin' pictures was tough. Only a few photographers ever really made it to the covers of magazines. The other ones set up studios in strip malls and took pictures of cute babies, kids graduatin' from high school, and couples havin' their 25th weddin' anniversaries. Liz sure didn't want to stay inside all day long and take portraits. If she was goin' to take pictures, she wanted to be on the move. She wanted to do it on her own terms, even though her own terms weren't payin' too many bills right now.

So, when Martin'd talked to her about the job, she told him she didn't have any experience but she'd give it some thought. She'd been trainin' to run a marathon 'round the same time he had and the two of 'em met at a runner's support group. Martin'd seen how Liz'd made everybody around her feel comfortable and thought she'd be able to help Pure Pet. After Martin told Liz the Pure Pet story, she decided she'd give it a shot. If she was goin' to do somethin' other than take pictures, she might as well be helpin' someone out. Besides, takin' pictures'd taught her to put people at ease. She got better pictures that way. And although she'd never sold anythin' a day in her life, she knew she could talk to just about anyone. So, when she finally made up her mind to take the job, she decided she'd do it just long enough to save money so she could take pictures full time. And yes, you can bet she'd be takin' that camera with her everywhere she went. She would, after all, be flyin' all over the country and seein' places she'd never seen before.

Jon

Jon Franklin'd been with CPI for quite a long time, and boy, was he burned out. The corporate grind'd finally started to get under his skin. He complained every night to his wife but what was he to do? One kid was startin' college in the fall and the other'd be startin' in two years. There was no way he'd be able to leave and retirement was still a long ways off. So, Jon got up every mornin', trudged off to work for eight hours or so and trudged back. The only thing that kept him goin' were his kids and he wasn't about to let either of 'em down, even if he'd have to suffer a bit with the constant memos from upper management about 'cuttin costs' and 'bottom lines'.

Jon managed a small department that dealt with product placement. His team designed eye-catchin' ways of displayin' product so folks'd stop and look. At one time, he'd liked the creativity, but over the years, store shelvin' hadn't changed much. In fact, the company'd started cuttin' jobs in his department and rumor had it that the whole department was goin' to get shut down, includin' Jon's position. He figured, since he'd started years ago with CPI in shippin' and distributin', that he'd be able to transfer back. To tell ya' the truth, he didn't really care one way or the other, as long as he had a job. So, when he'd heard that Pure Pet needed help, he asked for permission to jump ship for awhile. The Pure Pet project sounded like somethin' that might be a bit more challengin' and maybe even a bit more fun. Besides, he'd get to meet some new folks. The three founders sounded pretty interestin' and so far he liked what he'd heard about Pure Pet and its cause. He couldn't remember hearin' about too many corporations that were tryin' to do somethin' worthwhile.

After his first meetin' with Jennifer, who brought him up to speed on everythin', he met Ben, Nick, and Martin. Jon was hooked. These guys didn't do things the way CPI did 'em. The first thing Martin'd told him was to wear comfortable clothes – somethin' he told everyone on the team after he first met 'em. There was a whole lot of energy behind this project and a place for some creativity too. Jon'd been stuck overseein' his product placement department and approvin' diagrams for so long he'd forgotten what it'd been like to actually work on somethin' different. And sure, there were goin' to be problems that came with a new product, but that was part of the challenge behind it all.

ᘒ ⑥ ᘒ

Now I don't want ya' to get the wrong idea, of course there're more people involved with Pure Pet, but ya'd get lost in a sea of names and positions if I kept introducin' 'em to ya'. Let's just leave it at this, most folks who came Pure Pet's way jumped happily onto the ship and contributed a whole lot of positive energy towards the cause. So with that in mind, let's stick with the four folks I just introduced and see how things go. In fact, as I look forward at what might happen in the story, I don't believe we're going to get around to introducin' anybody else. I don't think there's goin' to be a need.

By the way, Martin, Nick, and Ben've pretty much served their purpose for my tellin' of the story. Sure, we'll still see 'em. They'll be at meetins'. They'll meet some important folks, and they'll show up at times when things might get a little sticky, times when they'll be forced to make a couple of important decisions and that'll be that. Ya' see, because this is a story about people, we need to take a look at a few others who took the guys' plan and made it work. These everyday ordinary folks might not be the visionaries that Martin, Nick and Ben are, but Pure Pet wouldn't've gotten anywhere without 'em. They're heroes too.

Chapter 23 ⑥

When our three guys arrived at the first production meeting after their move to CPI, they were introduced to some new members of the team. Howard stood up to greet them and had a difficult time hiding a frown. One of the guys standing before him wore jeans, flip-flops, and a floral printed shirt. Another wore cowboy boots, a cowboy hat, jeans, and a denim jacket. And the last one walked in wearing fine Italian leather shoes and an Armani suit. Howard didn't get it. Wasn't this supposed to be a business meeting?

Extending his hand , Howard introduced himself. "Mr. Trotter, Mr. Patterson, Mr. Pollard, I'm Howard Sands. I'm your liaison between Pure Pet and CPI. We're extremely excited to have you come on board."

"Please, Howard, we go by first names around here. I'm Ben, this is Martin, and this is Nick. In fact, I don't think I even knew what your last names were, guys." Everyone chuckled. Howard did so nervously.

"I'd also like you to meet Jennifer Billings." Jennifer was at the back of the conference room getting the supplies for the meeting in order. She walked up in her business suit with a welcoming smile when Howard said her name. "She'll be working with us on a part-time basis but she should be able to handle your inquiries in case I'm not available. I have several other projects I'm working on besides Pure Pet so Jennifer will be here if you need her."

"It's a pleasure to meet all of you," Jennifer said shaking hands. "I was reading a bit about Pure Pet last night. From what I can tell, you've put this thing together for the right reasons. There are a few farmers in my family background. I know they'll be pleased that I'm working on something to help them out."

"Well, we're glad to have you working with us," Martin smiled. "We're always looking for people who like what we do and can support it. We're ready to get rolling and get this stuff to the market. I'm sure we'll all get to know each other quite well. Now, first things first. If you're going to be working with us and keeping us connected to Howard, are you comfortable in that suit?"

"Excuse me?"

"Are you comfortable wearing that business suit?"

"As comfortable as someone can be wearing a business suit, I guess."

"Well, we ignore Ben most of the time. Apparently he likes stuffing himself in those fancy clothes every day but we sure don't. We're comfortable wearing what we're in. We want you to be comfortable when you're working with us. From here on out, when you meet with us, wear what makes you comfortable. By all means, if you're comfortable in a suit, wear it, but if you'd rather wear something else, do so."

"But I was told just last week that I shouldn't be wearing my bikini to work," Jennifer replied. Everyone laughed.

"Okay, no bikinis, but please, wear comfortable clothing," Martin replied. "And, I can see we might just need to hire you full time. There's always room for someone with a sense of humor."

"Gentlemen," Howard broke in abruptly. "Shall we get started?"

"Well, I guess that's why we're here," Nick said. "But before we get started, we need to explain something to everyone."

For the next 30 minutes or so, Nick, Ben, and Martin discussed the importance of the Pure Pet mission and the history behind the company. They stressed the importance of the cause and why everyone needed to be a committed member of the team. Everyone needed to be a part of 'Saving the Earth, one bag of dog food at a time.' Jennifer seemed to hang on every word. Howard looked bored and distracted.

꠷ ⑥ ꠷

How do ya' like that? Jennifer's payin' attention. Howard's not. The guy who's supposed to be the direct link's off in daydream land. Maybe he's already spendin' the money from the big promotion he thinks he's goin' to get. Maybe he's already out scuba divin' off the coast of Fiji. Who knows? But he sure isn't payin' attention.

Hmmm... I guess when I look at this situation, I've got to ask, "How in the heck do ya' get everybody on the team committed? How do you get everyone to believe in 'Saving the Earth, one bag of dog food at a time'? I mean, how do ya' take a bunch of people who're thrown in your lap, who you've been told're good people, and get 'em to follow ya'?" I'm not so sure I know the answer to my questions. Imagine that? Me, the all knowin' narrator, not knowin' the answer to my own darn question. I guess maybe sometimes it's okay to not to know all the answers.

By the way, we don't have to worry too much about Jennifer hittin' the ground runnin'. She's goin' to jump right in. And Liz? Well, even though we haven't seen her in action yet, she comes into this project with very little knowledge about what she's really gettin' herself into, but a whole lot of enthusiasm. And you know what? It probably works better for her that way because she doesn't know what to expect. Now Jon, he's another story. The poor guy's burned out. But he's got a big heart and a lot of drive if our guys can find a way to tap into it. I bet they'll find a way, even when it turns out that he's about to lose his position with the company. And Howard. Howard, Howard, Howard. You've probably been waitin' for me to get to Howard and I'm guessin' you've probably got a pretty good gut instinct about him. Howard just might have some problems gettin' his hands dirty in the right puddle of mud. But for now, I guess we'll just have to wait and see.

Chapter 24

To make sure that the product hit the store shelves by the launch date, Pure Pet went into overdrive just about the same time the first production meeting with Howard and Jennifer ended. Weekly meetings got the team geared up and moving each week. Monday mornings found everyone catching up on the past week and setting goals for the next week. As time went by, more and more people seemed to appear in the conference room each week. The team grew from the original 3 founders to over 20. Sales representatives, legal experts, marketing experts, formulation experts, you-name-it experts all showed up in some form or another. After each meeting was over, Martin, Nick, and Ben usually grabbed a cab to the airport and headed off in one direction or the other.

Nick spent most of his time making sure that natural meat sources would be readily available and that everything in the production process would be up and running in time. He met with researchers at Howell University who helped refine the Pure Pet formulas so that cats and dogs would actually eat it. He met with skeptical ranchers who didn't believe anything was going to happen until it did. And, he met with the plant managers to make sure they understood what Pure Pet was trying to do.

Martin and Ben, on the other hand, split their time hiring more team members, organizing a marketing and advertising strategy, and meeting with anyone who they thought might help them get the word out. Early on, Phil put in a call to Dr. Ball who, as it turns out, couldn't wait to meet Martin and Ben. She was so excited about Pure Pet that she invited them down to New Mexico for a weekend. After they returned from three relaxing days at Dr. Ball's ranch and several lengthy discussions ranging from the general health of the American public to the treatment of cattle at factory farms, the guys handed Nick an agreement stating that Dr. Ball would endorse Pure Pet products. Both of her retrievers had loved the sample food and it comforted her to know that she wouldn't have to continue to feed them foods that were made with by-products and hormone tainted meat. It was a major breakthrough for the guys. Pure Pet would gain immediate credibility in the marketplace with Dr. Ball's friendly face on each bag of food.

ॐ ⑥ ॐ

I know, I know, I told ya' that we weren't goin' to see Martin, Nick, and Ben much more, but I just had to mention this breakthrough. Besides, I kept it short and I'll keep this short. Ya' see, Dr. Ball touches a lot of people. Her approach to medicine starts with folks takin' good care of themselves by exercisin' and eatin' good, wholesome, fresh food. So, when it came to Pure Pet's mission, she saw the bigger picture. By supportin' family farmers who took care of the land there just might be a groundswell that steered folks towards organic food sections in the grocery store. And those folks might just start purchasin' better foods and leadin' healthier lives.

I guess what I'm gettin' at is that once ya' start lookin' around ya' never know who might pop up and believe in yer cause. I would've never mixed the medical profession in with a bag of dog food, but now I can see how they might work together. Who knows, as time goes by, how many other folks'll come to Pure Pet from different organizations with different interests that end up, somehow, bein' connected?

Chapter 25

On her first day, Liz Campos almost left the Pure Pet offices and headed back to the airport. She just wasn't sure she belonged. Her flight the night before had been uneventful but now, the girl who liked to hide behind a camera would soon be stepping in front of it. She would be the face of the company from the eastern side of the Rocky Mountains to the western side of the Appalachian Range – farm country. Other than four years on the east coast, Liz had lived in southern California her whole life and didn't quite know what to think. As she sat through her first meeting and soaked up all of the information, she began to think that she'd made the wrong decision. Part of the problem rested in the fact that Liz came from outside CPI. In fact, she'd never worked in an office before. She wasn't sure of office protocol or when she should talk in a meeting or who she should go to if she had questions. And here she was, sitting in a meeting with a bunch of people who sounded like they knew what they were talking about.

As the day wore on, despite the fact that she was captivated by all of the energy in the room, Liz talked herself out of the job. Before she headed back to her hotel for the evening, she spoke with Martin about quitting. She felt like a clueless outsider.

"Martin, I really don't think I can do this. I'm honored and touched that you thought that I could do this job, but I really don't think I have it in me."

"Sure you do. You can probably do this better than anyone who's been doing it for years. One of the reasons I came to you was because you're fresh. You don't have any preconceived notions about the way things are supposed to be. Pure Pet wants, no, needs fresh people. We don't want people who are stuck in their ways and do something a certain way. We want someone who is going to mess up from time to time, who turns around and learns from those lessons and keeps at it. I didn't ask you to take on this job because of your vast experience. I asked you because I like your energy. I like the way you interact with people. Besides, whenever I mentioned the company in passing, you always seemed genuinely interested. We need that. The rest of the stuff you can learn. You really just have to go out and be yourself. You can do that. You put people at ease. Just imagine that you want to take their picture each time you strike up a conversation."

"But, I really don't..."

Martin cut her off. "Listen, I'll tell you what. Give it one month. Take in as much as you possibly can. Meet with as many people as you can and if you still don't think you can do it, it's no big deal. We'll shake hands, remain friends, and still run together on Saturday mornings." Liz felt a bit better even though some uncertainty clung to her. She agreed to Martin's proposal.

"Alright. I'll see you tomorrow," Liz said.

"See you tomorrow," Martin replied. "Take some time this evening to let today sink in."

As it turned out, Liz never had the 30 day talk. Energized by the faith that Martin, Ben, and Nick had placed in her, Liz devoted herself to becoming an excellent representative. After her first handful of visits to retailers, Liz settled into a groove and even began looking forward to the visits. She met new people at each place. She traveled to new places and slowly came to the realization that a lot of good people lived everywhere she traveled. She also packed her camera with her wherever she went. She took pictures of everything.

Inevitably, Liz tripped on a few things along the way but she always managed to get back up, dust herself off, and keep at it. In fact, her lack of knowledge of "the rules" became an asset to her. She did things that seasoned representatives wouldn't have done. She asked questions that she didn't know she shouldn't ask. She was up front with everyone and took the time to get to know her clients. To her, it wasn't just a sales position. To her, each discussion became an opportunity to get more people involved in the cause. It hadn't taken her long to feed off of the energy of Pure Pet's mission. Her belief in the fact that she was doing something good for the world drove her to work even harder, sometimes working 12 to 15 hour days. In a short amount of time, the guys realized what an incredible asset she had become for the company. In fact, she had done such an awesome job that when the West Coast representative had to take a personal leave, she volunteered to fill in and cover both territories for a month.

There's somethin' about bein' the rookie that sure can carry people along. Rookies might not know much, but ya' know what?

Not knowin' much isn't always a bad thing. Havin' a lot of energy and motivation can sure make up for not knowin' much a lot of times. Shoot, most of us don't know much about a lot of things. We've all been rookies in some area of our lives. Liz's strongest asset walkin' into her job was not knowin'. Martin knew that. But, he liked her energy and he liked how she dealt with people. He knew she'd be able to talk to people even though she didn't know anythin' about sales or marketin' or pet food.

Ya' see, sometimes not knowin' brings with it a different point of view. It brings new ideas. It brings with it a complete lack of understandin' about "how things are and how things are supposed to be." And with Pure Pet, a company founded on breakin' rules and creatin' new norms, Liz was a perfect fit. And so were several other folks who Pure Pet hired from the outside. In fact, the guys made it a habit to hire folks without experience because they didn't want to have to spend a whole lot of time changin' people's habits and their minds. They also liked the fresh ideas that people brought along. So, as Pure Pet wobbled along as a toddler, so did Liz and several others.

Chapter 26

O ver the next couple of months, Pure Pet's ranks swelled. Many of the people who joined the team were thrilled to be doing something new and like Liz, became energized by the founders' enthusiasm towards the mission and the product. Jennifer found herself captivated by the dedication that Nick, Martin, and Ben brought with them to each meeting. She soon found herself putting in more time than she was being paid for. She began sharing her ideas regarding the product and marketing with the guys. She became much more involved than Howard, who, from the beginning, seemed to take a hands off approach to everything.

Howard was a fish out of water. Or a small fish in a bigger pond than he wanted to be swimming in. This group of "hired guns" that CPI had brought in didn't do things the way they were 'supposed' to be done and Howard had to deal with the fallout. Calls came in from CPI processing plants complaining that some guy named Nick Patterson, who claimed to be a Vice President of some new division, had showed up unannounced. Nick, unbeknownst to everyone but Ben and Martin, had been flying his single engine Cessna into little towns where CPI had plants in order to see how pet food was made. His curiosity had gotten the best of him. He wanted to know how things worked, and, since he had the time to do it and processing fell into his realm of responsibilities, Martin and Ben were all for it. The more he learned, the more they learned. Apparently, however, these unannounced meetings did not fit with CPI protocol. Visits by any sort of upper management were supposed to be arranged ahead of time so as not to frenzy plant managers.

There were more complaints too and Howard had to field them all.

"Who are these guys?"

"Don't they know how to behave?"

"We have policies in place for everything. Why is the CEO of the new division calling me for paperwork questions? Doesn't he know the proper channels to go through?"

Howard felt like things were spiraling out of control. He felt as though he was constantly putting out fires while everyone around him seemed to be deeply involved in this project. He felt left in the dark about a lot of things. This couldn't happen. After all, he was supposed to be the man in charge.

Jennifer, on the other hand, had taken on the role of general manager – not because anyone asked her to, but because she was doing a general manager's duties – and not because anyone gave her the title or a raise and benefits to go with it. She just happened to see stuff that needed to get done and she did it, just like she had done when she had worked before her children came along. She organized meetings and made sure everyone was up to speed with new developments. She became the 'go to girl' who seemed to thrive on the responsibility and her belief in the cause. The guys couldn't have asked for anyone better. And in taking on all of this responsibility, Jennifer unintentionally became a threat to Howard even though she was his assistant. And as someone who didn't like to feel threatened, he began trying to take back control. One morning, just as the day was getting started, he decided that his first action would be to knock Jennifer down a peg or two.

"Jennifer, this is Howard."

"Yes Howard. What can I do for you?"

"Jennifer, it seems that your responsibilities have grown."

"Have they? I just do whatever comes my way."

"Well, it seems like you're taking on too much. From here on out I need you to clear everything you're doing with me. I need you to send me a brief summary of all of the duties and responsibilities you've taken on. Also, if something new comes your way, contact me about it before you do anything."

"I'm really not having any trouble dealing with the workload, Howard. Won't this slow things down a bit?"

"Jennifer, you work here part-time. I've been doing this for a long time. I know what's best. Let's just leave it at that."

"Okay Mr. Sands. I hope I don't bug you too much with everything. Things only seem to get busier around here."

"Thank you Jennifer. I'll let you know if you're calling me too much."

Jennifer hung up the phone a bit puzzled. *Where did that come from?* she asked herself.

She shrugged her shoulders. *If he wants me to contact him for every little thing, I'll never get anything done and then what good will I be? Nick and Martin and Ben call me all the time to get stuff done. They depend on me. How will I be any good to the company if*

I'm calling Howard every single time someone asks me to do something? I just don't think he gets it sometimes. This thing is going to be big. There's work to be done to make it big. If he weren't so worried about following the rules all the time, maybe he'd get more done too. This just isn't going to work. I'm going to keep doing what I'm doing. I'll try to make myself less available to him.

Jennifer got up from her desk and took a short walk. She got herself a cup of coffee, said hello to a few folks and returned to her desk. She checked her email and saw 5 new messages in her inbox. Two were from Ben. Two were about distribution and one was from her mother. She answered them as quickly as possible and moved onto her next project.

⌀ ⑥ ⌀

Some people just don't get it, do they? Oh, they act like they want to get it, they pretend that they get it, but they never really do. They hide behind their own bluster or their "know-it-all-ness." They think everyone else around 'em's beneath 'em but they're the one's who don't really get the big picture. Howard sure doesn't get it and I'm not so sure he ever will. Short-sighted people like Howard always seem to be workin' some sort of angle. And it's usually an angle that turns suddenly and leads 'em down the wrong path.

When it comes right down to it, though, I'm not really here to complain about folks like Howard. I guess I'm here more to figure out what to do with him. I mean, what do ya' do when a guy or a gal like Howard starts causin' problems? If ye'r workin' with him or workin' for him, how do ya' deal with it? I guess ya' can do what Jennifer did. Keep yer nose to the grindstone and keep gettin' the stuff done that ya' need to get done. Or, I guess ya' could hand all of the work over to Howard and pretend ye'r completely swamped. That's kinda what he asked for, isn't it? The problem is, folks like Howard usually don't go away and folks like Jennifer get stuck tryin' to figure things out. Right now, she thinks she'll just try to avoid him as much as possible. I guess for now, you and me'll just have to wait to see how things work themselves out.

Chapter 27

At the main office, everyone had their eyes set on the launch date for the product. Marketing folks designed and redesigned packaging and advertising materials. Representatives flew around the countryside and talked with store managers about this new product. There was a buzz in the farm world that natural meat farmers had a new place to sell their meat. Everything was looking up. Everything was looking good. Jennifer continued to organize the weekly meetings even after she had sent her list of duties to Howard, who, incidentally, she hadn't heard a whole lot from since their discussion. After a few days, she had written it off as him having a bad day and forgotten about it. She hadn't been running any new tasks by him as she felt too busy to slow down. The work had to be done. Between her work at home and her work at the office, she didn't have a spare moment.

One Monday morning, after sending her kids off to school Jennifer rushed into the office, and prepared for a team meeting. Her mind was stuck on distribution. Pure Pet needed a distribution plan. The product was to be launched in 6 weeks or so and nobody had any idea how they were going to deliver everything to the places it needed to get to. As a few of the early birds started to wander into the conference room, Howard strolled up to Jennifer who was busily stapling handouts together for everyone.

"Jennifer, I need to speak with you."

"I'll have time after the meeting, Howard."

"You must've misunderstood me. I meant we need to speak right now."

"But the meeting's about to start. We've got to discuss distribution. We don't have a solid plan for getting this stuff out to the retailers. Right now is not a very good time. What's this about?"

"Put your things down. Take a deep breath and step out into the hallway with me for a minute," Howard replied sternly. "We'll talk about it out there."

Taking a deep breath and trying to keep her composure, Jennifer replied, "I'm leading this meeting and it begins in 10 minutes. I need to be able to run this meeting and keep everyone organized and on task. I am going to keep doing what I'm doing and then I will speak with you when I'm done. Unless one of my kids is bleeding or on the way to an emergency room, I think this can wait."

Jennifer turned her back on Howard and kept working. Taking a deep breath, she continued to greet people as they walked in the door and hand each one a stapled packet. Ben, who was perpetually early had sat quietly in the corner behind his laptop and watched the interaction between the two. He was puzzled by it and decided he'd find out what the problem was after the meeting. The last thing Pure Pet needed was turmoil in the ranks. He made a note to speak with Martin and Nick to see if they knew anything. Right now, however, everyone was taking their seats except for Martin who walked around the table shaking everyone's hands and telling them what a valuable asset they were to the team.

"Good morning everyone. I hope you all had a good weekend. I'd like to get started." Jennifer paused for a moment. "Everyone, say good morning to Martin." The crowd chuckled, Martin looked up and smiled and made his way to his seat.

"Hey, I'd just like to tell everyone that everything looks great. Ben and Nick and I are amazed at how much energy and time everyone's putting in. This is definitely going to be a huge success. And, while I'm at it, I'd like to offer a special thanks to Jennifer. She's keeping us all linked. Thank you Jennifer."

Jennifer smiled, "Thank you Martin. If we can look at our agendas today, you'll see that our top item to discuss is distribution. As you'll see, we really don't have a plan in place and we need to get one in place. We don't know how we're planning on getting our pet food out to the retailer. Has anyone given this any thought yet? I know we've all been busy, but I know this has come up a little bit from time to time."

When Jennifer asked who could pick it up from here, Jon jumped right in. "Well, I've thought about it a little bit, and I actually have a few ideas for distribution. As we worked on the store diagrams I got to thinking about getting the product out. The past couple of days I've been writing down ideas. Shall I continue?"

"By all means, please continue," Martin replied. "This is an issue we don't really have a clue about so if you do, let's hear it."

Jon began explaining his ideas for distribution. He had actually thought things through pretty clearly. His ideas, at least to the guys, all sounded feasible. They didn't really know how it was all supposed to work anyway. None of them had spent much time distributing anything other than their own ideas. Getting a product through production, into packaging, onto trucks and to retailers was a whole new realm for them. They were actually all pretty relieved that Jon had taken the reigns without even being asked, and come up with a plan.

"Jon, these all sound like feasible solutions. Can we count on you to head up the distribution of the product and let us know what you will need to get the job done?" Martin asked.

"Definitely. I'd be glad to do it," Jon replied. "Most of the display schematics are all ready to go. I've got some time."

"Great. Make sure Jennifer knows what your needs are and we'll make sure you get them," Martin said.

⌇ ⑥ ⌇

I know I'm jumpin' into the scene a little bit early here, but I have to. Ya' see, this is really the first time we've seen Jon in action. And just what do we see? Someone energized. Someone willin' to jump in and take the lead. Someone who seems just a little bit inspired. Isn't it refreshin'? You see, the cause's grabbed Jon by the hand and the two of them've been skippin' happily down pet food alley. It's the first time in several years that Jon hasn't groaned about goin' to work. Pretty neat, isn't it?

⌇ ⑥ ⌇

At the sound of Jennifer's name, Howard bristled. He had sat in the meeting watching everyone carefully, especially Jennifer who didn't seem to be bothered by their earlier discussion. She had deliberately defied him in front of others. Their next discussion would be a bit different than the one he had originally intended. Who did she think she was telling him to wait? Didn't she understand office protocol? He was her immediate boss, after all. And here she was getting another assignment from the guys without it coming through him.

"I'd like to interject something here," Howard interrupted. "I really think that Jennifer's plate is too full for another responsibility. Is there someone else who can work with Jon on the distribution end of things? Jennifer needs to be able to focus on other duties."

"I really don't mind, Mr. Sands. I can handle it," Jennifer replied curtly. She was embarrassed that he was making a deal of this in front of the team.

"I know that you think you can handle all of this, but I really think too much is already on your plate. We should find someone else," Howard said.

"I don't know who else we would get," Ben said. "Jennifer gets it done around here. If anything, we need to be paying her more and giving her benefits. Do you have someone else in mind, Howard?" Howard was taken off guard by Ben's question. He hadn't even thought of someone else. He was just trying to fluster Jennifer and let her know that he was still her boss. "Well, umm, I thought we could ask Jennifer who she thought could do the job. We can always bring in a temp if we need to."

"A temp? A temp to handle distribution of our product?" Nick sounded a bit agitated.

The conference room became silent. The 20 or so people in the room watched everything closely. "Jennifer, do you have anyone that will help you?"

"With all due respect to Mr. Sands," Jennifer replied, "I can get everything done."

"Then it's settled," Ben replied. "Jon, get a list to Jennifer of your needs. We'll take care of it. What's the next item on our agenda?"

The meeting moved on from there. Feeling as though he had just been slapped in the face, Howard excused himself about 10 minutes later and didn't return. He headed to his office where he began writing up an employee infraction sheet. Jennifer was going to get more than just a talking to. This would go into her permanent personnel file. Her defiance and insubordination would be duly noted. After he finished writing up the report and planning his discussion, he left a message on her phone and sent an email explaining that she should see him immediately after the meeting.

At 11 a.m. she still hadn't arrived at his office so he called one more time. No answer. He left his office and headed down the hallway towards the conference room where he found the meeting still in session. He crept in quietly and returned to his seat. If asked, he would say that he had gotten an urgent call from corporate. Just as he got himself comfortable, Jennifer thanked everyone for coming and adjourned the meeting. Everyone gathered their things and headed off into their respective roles. Jennifer stayed behind to clean up and to touch base with the guys. Howard, seeing that a small meeting was taking place, walked up and joined the conversation as if nothing had happened earlier.

"I'm sorry I missed some of the meeting. I had a call come in from corporate," Howard said a little too hastily. "Jennifer, when you're done here, will you stop by my office?"

"I'd be glad to stop by, Mr. Sands. I'll be there in a few minutes. Actually, you may be interested in what we're discussing," Jennifer replied.

"Sure. Sounds great. I probably need to be front-loaded with this stuff," Howard replied.

The tension between Howard and Jennifer was not lost to Martin, Nick, and Ben. Something was definitely up. When the meeting was over, Ben told the guys what he had seen earlier. He also offered to follow up and see what the problem was. It sure didn't seem like Howard was on the same page with everyone else. In fact, it didn't even seem like he was even in the same book.

Jennifer made her way to Howard's office with some trepidation. She didn't know what his problem was or why she was the target. The only thing she thought that could be behind his actions was jealousy. But what was he jealous about? She was doing the work. She was only getting paid part time. He was in management. His salary and benefits package was much higher than hers. What was his problem? Maybe the guys threatened him. Maybe their different approach to running things bothered him. But whatever it was, she was the target. She had just started to like what she was doing, too. She really didn't need this kind of grief.

"Mr. Sands, you asked me to stop by?"

"Yes Jennifer, come in. Sit down."

"Have I done something to offend you Mr. Sands?"

"I'll be doing the talking for this meeting, Mrs. Billings. And yes, you've done a thing or two. When I left the meeting today it was to come and fill out an employee reprimand form. You do understand what a reprimand is, don't you Mrs. Billings?"

"Mr. Sands, I don't know what I've done…" Howard cut her off.

"I must ask you to sit there and listen to what I have to say. A couple of weeks ago I…"

"Mr. Sands," Jennifer interrupted. "This is a part-time job. And as much as I like what I'm doing right now, I don't need this kind of treatment." Jennifer couldn't believe what was coming out of her mouth. Her old business instincts were kicking into high gear. It frightened her a bit and energized her at the same time. "As of now, I no longer work for CPI for Pure Pet or for anyone else. And I definitely don't work for you. I don't need this extra stress in my life. My family doesn't need me coming home a mess. This is not why I took this job, nor have I done anything that I feel is inappropriate. If I'm guilty of anything it's working too hard. Now, if you'll excuse me, I'll be leaving. Thank you very much and have a nice day."

With that, Jennifer got up from her chair, left the office and headed to her desk. She would be cleared out in no time. She didn't even care about receiving her next paycheck. She didn't need someone with an ego problem hounding her at work.

Howard was flabbergasted. *How dare she cut me off? How dare she not let me speak? How dare she quit on me?* Never in his career had someone walked out on him like this. He sat at his desk staring blankly at the picture on the wall in front of him.

ᔓ ⑥ ᔓ

Jennifer is about to leave the buildin', ladies and gentleman. Yes, Jennifer. I bet none of ya' saw that one comin'. Seems a bit sudden, eh? Maybe a bit, but maybe not. Things've been brewin' between those two for quite some time. And really, which one of you's goin' to side with Howard? Jennifer did the right thing, didn't she? If she's not goin' to look out for herself, who will? Oh, I just love watchin' her suck all the life out of Howard when she quits and storms out of his office. It's almost poetic. But ya' know, maybe we can all learn a bit from this situation. Maybe keepin' her nose to the grindstone and lettin' all this tension build up wasn't the best way for her to handle the situation. You see, she's an awfully important part of the Pure Pet machine right now. She knows what everyone is doin', how they're doin' it, and why. Besides, she really liked what she was doin'. Now, the cause is goin' to suffer as the guys scramble to find someone to fill her role.

Chapter 28

Ben had just finished speaking with Martin and Nick and begun making his way through the office. He figured that this was as good a time as any to speak to Jennifer and find out if there were any real problems. As he made his way across the office to her desk, he found her grabbing her purse and heading for the door. Ben was surprised. He thought maybe something was wrong at home.

"Jennifer? You're leaving early and you seem like you're in a rush. Is there a problem?" When Jennifer turned towards him it looked like she was almost in tears.

"Ben, I hope Pure Pet turns into something great. I'm sorry I won't be around to watch it succeed. I won't be working here anymore. I just quit."

Ben was in shock. *How can she just quit? She's our main support. She makes everyone around the office better. How can she just up an quit?* "Excuse me? You just quit?"

"Yes. I'm sorry, really I am. I just can't continue to work here, not with Mr. Sands. He seems to have some sort of problem with me. I just left his office after he showed me the employee reprimand sheet that he had filled out for me. I didn't even give him a chance to read it. I just quit. I don't need this. My kids don't need a stressed out mom, either."

"Why didn't you come and speak to us first?" Ben asked.

"Mr. Sands is my boss. Even though I've been working for you guys, he's still my boss. I didn't want to..."

Ben cut her off. "Hold on a second. You're not going anywhere. You just sit back down at your desk. We need you here. Better yet, go take a long lunch. Go home, see your kids. Come back this afternoon. You're not quitting. I've just made you our assistant. Do you have any idea how important you are to us and to getting this product up and running? We'd be two months behind schedule if it weren't for you. In fact, if you'll take the job full-time we'll pay you more, get you a benefits package, and officially make you General Manager of Pure Pet."

"I've already created enough waves. If I stayed it would just make things weird. I think I'd better go. Thank you anyway. And thank you for the kind words."

"Jennifer. I tell you what. Take the rest of the day off. Come back in the morning. I'm going to have a meeting with Martin and Nick right now to straighten this out. Things will be different in the morning, I guarantee you that. I'll check in with you later today. Leave your cell phone on."

"Thank you Ben. I'll think about it."

"Oh, you'll do more than think about it. You'll be back here tomorrow morning at 9 a.m. Now, go enjoy the afternoon off. And on top of that, I'm buying you lunch." Ben reached into his suit pocket, removed his wallet and handed Jennifer a hundred dollar bill. "Have a real nice lunch. And call your husband. See if he can meet you."

"Ben, I can't…"

"Yes, you can and you will. See you tomorrow." With that, he reached in his pocket for his phone. He hit the speed dial for Martin first. Nick would be next. And Howard? He'd see about Howard.

Later that evening, Jennifer received a call. She could see that it was from Martin. She picked up immediately.

"How's our new General Manager?" Martin asked.

"Hello Martin. Things got a bit messy today didn't they?"

"They were only a tiny bit messy when you left. They got even messier later. When you arrive tomorrow morning, your desk won't be in the same place. We've had it moved to an office that was recently vacated. You'll need an office now and not a cubicle."

"But I haven't even said I'm coming back."

"As far as Pure Pet is concerned, you never left. And, you've earned the position as General Manager. It is, after all, essentially what you've been doing since you started working with us."

"But what about Mr. Sands? Things are going to be weird and uncomfortable."

"You're moving into Howard's old office."

"You fired him?"

"No, Howard wasn't fired. He still works for CPI but his job position has changed. It no longer involves working with Pure Pet."

"But…"

"No buts, Jennifer. Howard was never really on our team. He never really cared about Pure Pet, the mission, and our cause. He had his own interests at heart and you threatened him because

you were doing such an outstanding job. You worked more closely with us than him and he didn't like it. He wanted to have it his
way and his way just won't work with Pure Pet. You see, Pure Pet
is bigger than him."

"Martin, thank you. I really didn't want to leave. I just…"

"We know Jennifer. We'll see you in the morning. And we
know that you still need to be there for your kids. Your new position will remain as flexible as your old one. Now, go be with your
family."

ↄ ⑥ ↄ

Oh, now, don't be upset with me. It was kinda fun givin' ya' a little
scare. No, Jennifer's not goin' anywhere and ol' Martin hit the nail
on the head. Ya' see, Martin, our everyday, ordinary person who
visited that strawberry patch a long time ago, would be the first
to agree that Pure Pet's bigger than him. It's bigger than all of us.
The Pure Pet story's compellin' because it isn't just about dog and
cat food. Sure, it's about helpin' farmers, but ultimately it's about
the world outside. By helpin' the farmers, the world becomes a
better, healthier place. There's the potential to have a tremendous
ripple effect. So, when it comes down to it, there just isn't any
room for negativity. Negativity's like a nasty ol' virus. One negative person can contaminate a whole office full of people. And in
Pure Pet's case, that just couldn't happen. Our everyday, ordinary
people had to be able to devote their energy towards the positive.
And that's why Howard didn't fit. He just couldn't seem to see the
big picture.

Now, to be quite honest with ya', I'm not sure it's all his fault.

In fact, I think we need to give ol' Howard the benefit of the doubt. Ya' see, the man's worked under strict corporate guidelines his whole career. He's been taught that there's a way to do things and a way not to do things. And, for the most part, he's played by the rules. So, I guess ya' gotta wonder what he's thinkin' when Martin, Nick, and Ben show up flyin' by the seats of their pants and preachin' comfy clothes. Howard couldn't tell which end was up and quickly became the 'fish out of water', 'the ol' dog who couldn't be taught new tricks'. I mean, Howard's not a bad guy. He and Pure Pet simply didn't fit. And even though most of us want things to work out perfectly, they can't always. Sometimes the only solution for those involved is to part ways.

Chapter 29

The next 6 weeks or so flew by. Everyone at Pure Pet prepared for the product launch. Ranchers had finally gotten their natural meat to Pure Pet plants. The plants were making the food. Representatives had flown up and down the east and west coasts and throughout the midwest getting grocery store managers prepared. Marketing had focused on the store front advertising materials. Distributors were making sure they had a way to get the stuff to the stores. Everyone was busily doing something. The excitement grew daily. Problems were dealt with easily and everyone seemed to smile at Pure Pet headquarters. They all knew that what they were doing was for a greater cause and because of that, everyone worked hard.

Jon Franklin sat on several bags of dog food behind a beat up old folding table equipped with only his laptop computer and a telephone. Surrounding him were pallets of Pure Pet product, signs for stores, and boxes of informational brochures. Call after call after call had come in.

"Where's this?"

"Where's that?"

"We don't have any of our food yet. How are we going to stock our shelves properly?"

Jon managed to take care of all of them. At one point he had gotten so busy that he began giving out his personal cell phone number also. He told customers, "Use this if the other line is busy." And they used it.

The past few weeks, Jon and his small team had worked with Jennifer to create a nationwide distribution system. The system tracked shipments, used state-of-the-art customer optimization programs, and had automatic reorder options built into it so that a store manager could order directly from Pure Pet. It worked beautifully. They'd done a final test run earlier that morning, the Friday before the first store set. They knew they'd cut it close but they'd gotten it done. What they hadn't thought of, however, was a distribution center. They'd spent so much time with the software system, they'd forgotten that they needed a distribution center. At the moment, all of the Pure Pet product and all of the advertising that needed to be to stores in the next few days sat on pallets in a small unused CPI warehouse. After it had all been produced, there had been no other place to put it so that's where the plant manager had sent it. It still sat there waiting.

In a short meeting after the software system had been checked, Jon and Jennifer met quickly to run down the list of things that needed to be done.

"We've got the system working. What else needs to be done today?" Jon asked.

"Well, who on your team is shipping everything out?" Jennifer asked.

"Who is shipping everything out? I....well...That's a good question. That's a very good question. I'm not sure I have an answer to that right now. I've been so wrapped up in getting this system ready that I hadn't actually thought about real product."

"Jon, we have our first store set on Wednesday. We have to get all the signs and all the product to that store by 6 a.m. on Wednesday morning. In fact, it should've been there already. You don't have anyone on your team working on this?"

"It's only been the three of us and there've been so many software glitches that…"

"Okay, it doesn't matter," Jennifer said taking a deep breath. We've dealt with problems before. We'll deal with this one. In fact, we'll deal with this one before we deal with anything else, and, we'll do it with a smile. We only have a few stores that are launching next week. Let's focus on them first." Jennifer smiled. She had worked here long enough to know they'd find a solution and that everything would work. That was one of the best things about working at Pure Pet. Maybe everything wouldn't work as smoothly as they'd all envisioned it, but things always worked out. It was hard for her to put her finger on it, but it was true. Maybe it was because everyone was so excited about the product. Maybe it was because everyone was so devoted to the cause. Whatever it was, she knew the product would get to the store, the signs would get to the store, and the launch would go. Everything would turn out fine.

"Seeing as how I'm supposed to be in charge of distribution, I suppose I should know the answer to this question, but, where's the product?" Jon asked.

"It's in a small unused CPI warehouse over off of 17th Street," Jennifer chuckled. "The factory manager sent it there because he didn't know what to do with it. I spoke with him earlier today."

"Okay, I'll get over there as soon as I can and see what things look like. I'll let you know what I need as soon as I have the situation evaluated. I'm taking my laptop. It has a copy of the distribution system on it."

Jennifer smiled. "Jon, the system test went well. It's just a matter of getting the product out now. We'll get it where it needs to go. It'll all work out. Don't try to do all of this on your own. Why don't you take the rest of the team with you?

"I can't. They'll have to be here if something goes wrong with the system."

"Okay, but don't kill yourself. Things always work out with Pure Pet. Don't forget the bigger mission."

"I won't forget. That's why I've stuck around so long. I'd better get going. If Martin, Ben, or Nick call, have them call me on my cell phone. Oh, and just for sanity's sake, let's try and make this look like it was all planned and that we have it all under control." Jon chuckled. "I'm sure they'll buy that!" With that, Jon headed to his desk, unplugged his computer, stowed it in his bag and headed for the door. It was Friday just before lunch. In the next week, Jon would make it home after his wife and kids were asleep and leave before everyone got up.

At the warehouse, Jon had found the product stacked in no particular order on pallets right inside the main door of the warehouse. He found a warped folding table and no chair. He improvised with a stack of dog food and set to work. Luckily, he had thought to stop by the technical support office and get a phone that he could plug into the company's network, just in case. Everything was going to work, he kept telling himself. Everything was going to work.

When ye'r suddenly inspired, sometimes work conditions don't really matter, especially when ye'r burned out and need a change. At the warehouse, Jon didn't mind the cement floors. He didn't mind the cool temperature, the lack of an office, or desk, or any of the other comforts you might imagine he's used to. Findin' an old wobbly foldin' table and stackin' some dog food bags to make a chair worked well enough for Jon. He had work to do. And it was the kinda' work that he smiled about and did happily. By the end of next week, Jon'll be tuckered out completely and runnin' on adrenaline and caffeine. But boy, would he have a good time doin' it.

He didn't even mind when his boss from his old departmen-t'd called and told him that she was comin' for a meetin'. He was, after all, really just on loan to Pure Pet. Jon also knew that the meetin'd probably serve one purpose – to inform him that his old department'd been permanently closed and that his position'd been terminated. Months ago, he'd heard through the grapevine that his position was in jeopardy. It was one of the reasons he volunteered to work with Pure Pet, a project he'd come to admire and a place where he was havin' fun. In fact, he liked workin' with Pure Pet so much he'd even decided he'd do it for free for a while if he had to. These bags and cans of food were goin' to get where they needed to get if he had anythin' to do with it. Besides, maybe losin' a job he really didn't like anymore would turn out to be a blessin' in disguise.

Chapter 30

The following week, on a busy Wednesday afternoon, Liz Campos, prepared for her first store set. After a whirlwind education into retail marketing and sales, countless flights around the country, and a month of sleepless nights heading into the product launch, Liz sat in her rental car listening to the radio, staring at a newly built grocery store that would open tomorrow. And when it opened, the first glimpse the outside world would have of an array of Pure Pet products would be sitting in full view. In appreciation for all of her hard work, Martin, Nick, and Ben, had decided that Liz had earned the right to set up the first store. When they informed her of this decision, she tried to talk them out of it. She still felt inexperienced and incapable, besides, this was the first time anyone would ever see Pure Pet products and Liz had never completed a store set before. She wasn't so sure she wanted that responsibility. After a short discussion, however, the guys assured her that she was more than ready to handle it. Besides, they told her, she had earned it.

So, here she sat, the warm sun beating through the windshield, leafing through pages of diagrams that showed how to organize everything. *What have I gotten myself into?* she asked herself. *The rest of this day is going to be crazy. I sure hope the people I'm meeting here know what to do. I'm not even sure I know how to read this product diagram.*

Inside the store, an empty aisle of shelving sat waiting to be organized, labeled, and stocked. Signs had to be hung, Pure Pet brochures had to be made available, and all of it had to be done according to the plans that Liz had been given. Each and every can and bag that would find its way onto the shelving had to be placed in an exact spot. Liz had never realized that grocery stores use schematic layouts for all of their goods.

Liz set herself a goal of three hours. If she could get everything done in that time frame, it would allow her a few minutes to relax and get a bite to eat before the evening started. Her day was far from over. After the aisle was stocked, she had to attend the grand opening party for the store. It would be a "meet and greet" opportunity for Liz to get to know other folks in the grocery industry along with the senior management of the store chain. Social events hadn't been something she had done very often as part of her job, so she was a bit excited about the evening. The party would be a great opportunity to spread the Pure Pet story. Besides, it would be a nice change of pace. A lot of people who worked hard to get this store open would attend. It would definitely be a celebration.

Taking her last sip of coffee, Liz breathed deeply, looked at her watch, got out of her car, and headed into the store. Crossing the parking lot, she called and left a message for Jennifer to let her know that she was there. The real work was about to begin. Pure Pet was about to be introduced to the world and she hoped, along with everyone else in the company, that it would be embraced by the consumer.

Waiting inside the store were a couple of people who Liz would come to rely on for the next few hours. They worked in CPI's grocery division and were there to help her get the aisle organized. Thankfully, they had done this before because as soon as she got a look at the empty cavern of an aisle, a lump grew in her throat. Glancing at her watch, she still hoped her three hour window of time would be enough.

Over the course of the past couple of days, Liz had called Jennifer every couple of hours to check and double check the list of things that she would need. At one point, after her fourth or fifth call, Jennifer told her she wasn't allowed to call back until Wednesday unless there was an emergency. Jennifer reassured Liz that everything would be at the store by Wednesday morning. Jon had sent everything on Friday afternoon. It would be there. But when Liz met with the store manager she was informed that nothing from Pure Pet had arrived. Liz excused herself and called Jennifer in a panic.

"Jennifer, this is Liz. This is an emergency."

"Liz, what's the problem? Did someone get hurt? Is everyone okay?"

"Yes, everyone's okay. What's not okay is the fact that nothing that Jon sent has arrived. I thought you told me it would be here by this morning."

"What do you mean? It was supposed to be delivered this morning at the latest. In fact, Jon told me he sent it guaranteed."

"Guarantee or no guarantee, nothing is here and I need this stuff now. I don't have much time and this store opens in a little over 12 hours. We can't have bare shelving when this store opens tomorrow. It's not like I can improvise on this one. I need the product." Liz's voice rose as she talked.

"Alright, I'm going to call Jon. I will call you back immediately with an answer. Hang on. I'm sure we'll get this worked out." Jennifer said reassuringly.

"Better yet, have Jon call me. I need this stuff as soon as possible. I've got people here waiting to help."

As soon as Liz hung up the phone she began pacing. Thank goodness she was in an organic food store that didn't sell cigarettes. She might decide to pick up an old habit. Within a matter of minutes, her cell phone rang. It was Jon.

"Liz, it's Jon. I'm sorry this happened. The truck picked up all of the stuff for your store last Friday and the company guaranteed it would be there no later than this morning. In fact, it should have been there yesterday. Listen, I called the shipping company. Yesterday, the driver got the name of the town you're in confused with a town that is 60 miles north of you. When he couldn't find the store it was too late to turn around and a severe weather forced him to spend the night up there. He left this morning around 8 a.m. He should've been there with the stuff. I'll call the shipping company back as soon as I get off the phone with you. They said if he's not there that he should be there in a short amount of time. Sit tight. I'll call back in a minute."

"Thanks Jon. I need this stuff now. Is there anything else we can do? Are there other stores around here that have already received stuff for their store sets later this week?"

"Unfortunately not. Your stuff was sent out first. The rest of the stuff is still in transit. You'll just have to wait. I'll call you right back."

Why don't things ever go the way they are supposed to? Liz asked herself. *If I had a dollar each time something like this has happened in my life I'd be able to retire now.* Liz continued to pace. Deciding it might be best to go outside and get some fresh air, she informed her CPI assistants that the truck was on its way and that she would return shortly. If anything showed up, they were to start bringing it to the aisle. Once outside, Liz's phone rang. She groaned when she saw it was Martin. She didn't want to let him down.

"Liz, it's Martin."

"Things sure get around quickly. Why are you calling?" she snapped.

"Lighten up a bit Liz. I'm not calling for any other reason than to let you know that everything's going to be okay. Jennifer said you sounded a bit stressed. We know you'll handle it and we know the stuff will get there and everything will be okay. We just want you to know that we have faith in you and that we know it will all get taken care of. Now, as you're doing all of this, don't forget to have some fun and don't forget to take a bunch of pictures for our offices."

"But Martin, how can I lighten up when I can't get anything…" Martin cut her off.

"Listen, we've all put a lot of time and energy into this project. If we have to wait one more day for everything to get off the ground, so be it. Nobody's going to die because our pet food isn't on the shelves. Besides, it'll show up today. Now, go have fun. We'll talk to you later."

Martin's call managed to accomplish its goal. It got Liz to look at things a bit more objectively and it helped to calm her down. By the time she hung up the phone, she felt better. *Martin's right. This isn't the most important thing in the world right now. If things get postponed for a day, no one's going to suffer. Besides, the stuff will get here, I know it will.*

꒜ ⑥ ꒜

Alright, everyone, let's all take a step back with Liz. Let's all take a deep breath. Here I go again jumpin' into the middle of the scene, but I need to take a little breather. Things're gettin' a bit tense. Thank goodness Martin called to calm things down. As if this story needed anythin' else to go wrong.

Ya' know, Martin's right. The world wasn't comin' to an end if their pet food didn't hit the shelves for one more day. No, there might not be the spectacular introduction that everyone was hopin' for, but in the end, everythin'd be okay. The farmers'd still sell their meat to Pure Pet, who'd still make the pet food and get it to the stores, who'd still sell it to the consumer. Shoot, after a couple of years of plannin', what's one more day? The funny thing is, we all get caught in this trap from time to time. Each of us gets so caught up in our own little parts of the world that we often forget to look at the bigger picture. In fact, that's been the wonderful thing about tellin' the story of Pure Pet. These guys started a company because of the bigger picture, and in the end, it's all goin' to work just fine, in spite of a minor shippin' problem or two.

꒜ ⑥ ꒜

By the time Liz got herself back into the store, she found the folks from CPI carting Pure Pet products into the aisle. The truck had arrived at the loading dock while she was out front and everything could get rolling. She let out a deep breath, smiled, and looked at her watch. They were starting an hour late. *No big deal,* she told herself. *What's an hour?* Relieved, she put in a quick call to Jennifer, let her know they were getting started, and told her that she'd email the digital photos of everything just as soon as the shelves were stocked and organized.

ᔔ ⓖ ᔔ

Well folks, our journey's just about come to an end. Sure, there're other stores that'll get their Pure Pet products, but it'll all happen without too many glitches. As it turned out, Liz and her crew got everythin' set up and in order. It took 'em about twice as long as they'd expected, but heck, when does a project ever take less time than you think it will to get done? Especially one you've never done before? It sure doesn't happen at my house, that's for sure.

By 8 o'clock that evenin', Liz shook hands with her team, took pictures of the first ever display of Pure Pet products, and headed to her hotel. She still had a party to get to and even though she was goin' to be a bit late, she wasn't goin' to miss it for the world. After a quick trip to the hotel to freshen up, Liz arrived at the party and walked up to the guest table.

"Hello, may we help you?" a friendly young man in a white coat and tie asked.

"Yes. My name is Elizabeth Campos. I'm a little late, but I'm with Pure Pet Foods."

"We're glad you could make it this evening, Ms. Campos. We also have a message for you. Can you wait here for just one minute? I'll be right back."

"Sure. Do you know what the message is about?"

"I'm afraid I don't," replied the young man. "I'll be right back."

A message? A message? Liz asked herself. *Why wouldn't someone call me on my cell phone? I hope there's not a problem at the store.*

"Excuse me, Ms. Campos. I have a message for you." a deep voice from behind her asked.

"Yes?" Liz answered turning around.

"We'd like you to join us at our table."

Standing before her were Martin, Nick, and Ben dressed in suits. Each of them had big smiles on their faces. "But, what are you guys doing here?" Liz asked as the smile on her face grew.

"You didn't think we'd miss this, did you?" Martin replied.

"Yeah, but you were supposed to be..."

"Right here. That's where we're supposed to be," Nick said. "Are you kidding us? Pure Pet goes on sale tomorrow morning. We have to be there and we figured since we had to be there tomorrow morning that we might as well come and celebrate with you."

"So you were here when I was freaking out earlier today?" Liz asked.

"Yep. We had a long lunch when Jennifer called us. She thought we might need to come and put out a fire or two. We talked about it for a minute or two, but we figured you could handle it. It looks like you did." Ben said.

"I'm so glad to see you guys. I've been looking forward to this evening but I had wished someone else would be here. I can't believe you came. Have you been to the store?"

"Everything at the store looks great. We popped in before we came here. We can't wait to see people's response." Nick said.

"So, would you like to sit at our table, or what?" Martin asked. "Let's go have some fun."

And with that, four smiling, everyday, ordinary people turned and headed into the party.

ᕽ ⑥ ᕽ

How d'ya' like that? Our guys'd been plannin' that all along. After they'd told Liz that she was goin' to take care of the first store, they'd decided to surprise her at the party. Don't ya' just love surprises sometimes?

The followin' mornin', the guys'd rise early, take Liz to breakfast and get to the store a little while before it opened. Once they got there, they waited around to meet some of the store's first customers and see what they thought about Pure Pet. It'd be the only time in the next couple of weeks that any of 'em would be able to enjoy their hard work. After all, there were other cities to fly to and a whole bunch of other store sets to get done.

Epilogue

Throughout the entire process of creatin' Pure Pet, one thing always rang true. The only reason the guys got as far as they did was because of the people who're involved. Sure, the idea was great, and the cause was definitely important, but none of it would've gotten anywhere without the people. People who're willin' to take risks. People who're willin' to earn less money. People who wanted nothin' more than to see the cause succeed, and not because it might turn 'em a profit, but because it was the right thing to do. Because they too, like the small, independent farmers, had families of their own. Because they too, felt it was important to offer the general public healthier food. Because they too, wanted the land to be available for generations to come.

Now I hope ya' don't mind, but I'd like to take one last look at everybody. It won't take but a minute, but I don't think I can finish the story if I don't give all of 'em one last little bit of attention. So please, bear with me. Besides, they're all pretty interestin' everyday, ordinary folks.

Take one last look at Nick. Nick hated to see animals raised the way they're bein' raised on factory farms. It made him sick to his stomach. He'd seen corporations without a conscience beat up on family farms, on the land, and on livestock for too many years. Nick knew there was a better way. A much better way that offered a good life to his friends, his family, and to all the other everyday, ordinary people.

And what about Mark? His organizin' and plannin' forced Pure Pet to grab Phil Lankford's attention. Mark was a drivin' force behind the company's original principles and mission. He'd been the one to draft the business agreement on the napkin. Remember? And a believer? Ya' might say that. Havin' already brought one organic company to life, here he was doin' the same thing again. The cause definitely meant somethin' to him.

Now Ben? Well, he jumped right into the middle of things and hit the ground runnin'. He saw the importance of the cause and supported it selflessly, pickin' up right where Mark left off. His ability to pitch the idea and come up with ideas for marketin' was one of the main reasons the guys had their meetin' with Phil Lankford. And when it finally came time to sell the idea to CPI? Well, what's there really to say?

And of course, we can't forget about li'l ol' Martin standin' in the strawberry patch. His unrelentin' pursuit of the cause drove the project from the get go. He never let up, even when he ran into one dead end after another. I guess there was somethin' that always told him everythin'd turn out alright.

And Phil? Phil never really worked with Pure Pet officially, but his broad thinkin' caused our boys to contact other folks who'd be drawn to help the cause – Howell University's research veterinarians, and of course, Dr. Ball. And we can't forget, without the money from Phil, Pure Pet would've had to close its doors and everyone would've been lookin' for somethin' new to sink their teeth into.

Next came Theresa. She floated into our story just for a minute, but without her, the deal with CPI would've never taken place. The guys'd still be lookin' for a processin' plant. And, if ya' remember, she did it all out of the goodness of her heart. She just wanted t'see the cause make it.

And who could forget the folks at CPI? Sure, they're a big corporation, but sometimes we tend to forget that there're a lot of everyday, ordinary folks workin' for those companies. And it's a good thing. The president gave the guys, and the cause, one heck of an opportunity.

Jennifer made the dream come true once it got up and runnin'. She was the glue that held everythin' together. Havin' seen the big picture from her first meetin' with the guys, Jennifer worked and got things done. And don't forget, she only worked part-time for the first six months.

Which I suppose leads me to Howard. When it comes down to it, I guess there ain't much to say about Howard that hasn't already been said.

And Jon, burned out Jon? Jon got everythin' organized so it'd get to the stores. Nothin' would've mattered much if the product never made it to the stores. And he did it all sittin' on stacks of dog food in a lousy, old, dusty warehouse without anyone's help. Oh, and by the way, I think I forgot to mention, Jon's boss never showed up. She didn't call. She didn't email. She just didn't show up. Now isn't that kinda rude? Apparently, after speakin' with our boys, Jon's division president called his boss and told her to leave his position alone.

And last, but definitely not least, Liz and the other sales reps became the face of good ol' Pure Pet. They shook hands, talked about the product, and got their hands dirty workin' in stores across the country. Within the first two weeks, they helped get Pure Pet in close to 100 stores. Without Liz and the rest of the team's belief in the cause, it would've never gotten done.

ॐ ⑥ ॐ

Well, I suppose that about covers it. I think I need to go get myself a glass of water. I'm a bit parched from talkin' so much. But before I go, here's a few things for ya' to think about. The cause that everyone in this story's workin' for still needs a lot of support. Heck, maybe somebody out there'll be inspired enough by this little tale to start up their own version of Pure Pet. That'd sure be nice.

But more importantly, let's not forget, there's still a quite a few farmers scattered across the countryside who need help. There's still a lot of animals bein' treated poorly. And, there's still a lot of tasty organic food to be eaten. I sure do hope the next time ya' head on over to the grocery store, some of this'll stick with ya'. I know it's stuck with me. It wouldn't hurt any of us to eat better food, live healthier lives, and smile knowin' we're helpin' out because of it. And I suppose, it just might not hurt to get yer pets involved either.

Appendix

Here're a few organizations ya' might like to take a look at. We sure like 'em. They do some mighty fine work.

Farm Aid

Farm Aid sure does put on some wonderful concerts, don't they? They sure do a whole lot more than that too. Farm Aid works to get farmin' back to bein' run by families. They work to support small family farms. They'd like to see an entire countryside of family farmers workin' to bring healthy food to the market, keep the land safe, and re-energize a whole lot of small communities. They'd love it if ya' stopped on by for a visit at:

www.farmaid.org

Farm Aid
11 Ward Street, Suite 200
Somerville, MA 02143
800-FARM-AID

The Organic Center for Education and Promotion

The fine folks at the Organic Center for Education and Promotion work to get more everyday, ordinary people to eat organic food. They work to educate us all about the healthy benefits of eatin' organics. They also work with other folks who spend quite a bit of time doin' scientific research about organic foods. They use all that research to help educate the media, government agencies, and all of us who make up the general public. For a more detailed account of what the fine folks at the Center do and to update yourself on the benefits of leadin' an organic lifestyle, please visit them at their website:

www.organic-center.org

The Organic Center for Education and Promotion
46 East Killingly Road
Foster, RI   02824

Association of Family Farms

The Association of Family Farms (AFF) is workin' hard to help family farms in the United States thrive and prosper. The good folks with AFF are designin' a marketin' system that brings local and regional family farm organizations together under a national "umbrella" brand. This brand'll enable family farms to produce wholesome foods and prosper. And, as they're growin' this great food, they'll take care of the land, treat animals humanely, and look after their communities. Please visit them at their website:

www.associationoffamilyfarms.org

Association of Family Farms
6741 Sebastopol Ave. Suite 220
Sebastopol, CA 95472
(707) 823-6111

Fundraising Efforts

Net proceeds from the sale of How Dog Food Saved the Earth will be donated by ASM Books to organizations that work to save family farms, promote sustainable and organic agriculture, and work to ensure the humane treatment of animals. To learn how you can help, for more information on these efforts and/or to see a list of organizations we support, please visit us on the web.

www.howdogfoodsavedtheearth.com

AUTHORS' PAGE

*K*ory Swanson

Kory Swanson's spent the past 14 years wanderin' the halls of good ol' public education remindin' students to dot their 'I's and cross their 'T's. After coaxin' kids to put words down on paper and revise, revise, revise, he finally decided it was about time to put his money where his mouth is.

Right about now, Kory's probably chasin' his toddler, Cole, around the house while his beautiful wife, Jennifer, brings home the bacon. Between naps you'll find him sittin' at the computer, tryin' to get more words to organize themselves on the computer screen.

This is the second time Kory's teamed up with Anthony. Take a look at The Detachment Paradox: The Workbook that Jennifer Todd, Anthony, and he wrote together.

*A*nthony Zolezzi

Anthony Zolezzi's spent the past 25 years workin' in the food industry, specializin' in new business development for the organic and natural food categories.

Zolezzi's a former board member of the Organic Alliance and a foundin' board member of the Organic Center for Education and Promotion. He's also on the leadership team of the Association of Family Farms, an initiative to organize family farms and sell products direct from the farm to retail and foodservice. Zolezzi's responsible for over 25 new product innovations and industry developments workin' with organizations rangin' from start-ups to Fortune 500 companies includin' Nestlé, Bumble Bee Seafood, The New Organics Co., Horizon Organic Dairy, Wild Oats Markets, Veg Fresh Farms, Sizzler International, Jack-In-The-Box Franchise, Eco Terra Development Co., C.H. Robinson, Bull & Finch Pub Enterprises, Cascadian Farms and Hidden Villa Ranch. In addition to his marketin', manufacturin', and distribution expertise, Zolezzi's taken social trends and turned 'em into food trends such as his creation of Bubba Gump Shrimp Co. Restaurants based on the award winnin' movie, Forrest Gump. He also developed Café Nervosa Coffee based off NBC's hit sitcom, Frasier.

Zolezzi's frequently called on as a health food expert by national media, includin' NBC's, Today show and national magazines, Time, and Newsweek. He also helps companies and individuals become more innovative and engaged in life and business by creating toxic-free corporate environments. Zolezzi is co-author of the book, Chemical-Free Kids (Kensington/Twin Streams, 2003), author of, The Detachment Paradox (ASM Books, 2004), and co-author of, The Detachment Paradox: The Workbook (ASM Books, 2005)

OTHER TITLES BY ASM BOOKS

The Detachment Paradox:
How an objective approach to work can lead to a rich and rewarding life

Feel like a 'Prisoner of Work'? Here are seven keys to set yourself free without having to quit your job.

Your job is supposed to be what you do for a living. Yet, increasingly, employers act as if your job is your primary purpose in life. As a result, we tend to not only lose contact with our family and friends, but we also lose a sense of who we are.

So, rather than take that job and shove it, you can instead take that job and rise above it. All you have to do is take a more objective approach to your work

The Detachment Paradox:
The Workbook

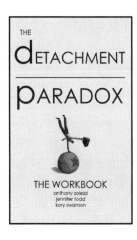

Our workbook is filled with exercises that will help you to transform your life both on and off the job.

Whereas the book, The Detachment Paradox, contains personal anecdotes and a thorough discussion of Anthony Zolezzi's seven keys to detachment, this workbook is filled with hands-on activities designed to get you moving and working towards a better life.

Zolezzi's seven keys, converted here into thoughtful activities, allow you to implement changes in your life as soon as you put your pen or your pencil down.

For further information or to order books,
please contact:

ASM Books

P.O. Box 3083
La Habra, CA 90631
(310) 528-2830

www.asmbooks.com
info@asmbooks.com

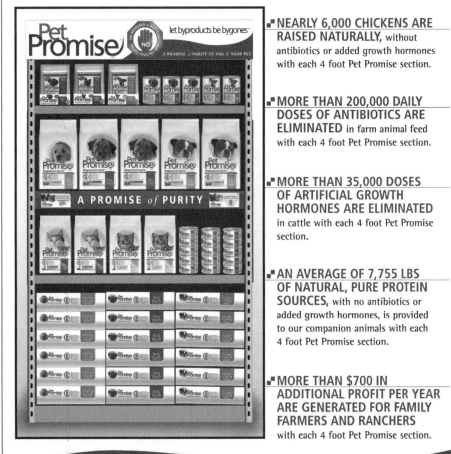